Developing as a Secondary School Mentor

Developing as a Secondary School Mentor:

A Case Study Approach for Trainee Mentors and their Tutors

Alan Child and Stephen Merrill

LearningMatters

Learning Resources
Centre

12787876

First published in 2005 by Learning Matters Ltd.

British Library Cataloguing in Publication Data
A CIP record for this book is available from the British Library

ISBN 1 84445 026 0

Cover and text design by Topics – The Creative Partnership
Project Management by Deer Park Productions
Typesetting by Pantek Arts Ltd, Maidstone, Kent
Printed and bound in Great Britain by Bell & Bain Ltd, Glasgow.

Learning Matters Ltd
33 Southernhay East
Exeter EX1 1NX
Tel: 01392 215560
E-mail: info@learningmatters.co.uk
www.learningmatters.co.uk

Contents

Introduction 1

1 What is a mentor? 11

2 Picking up the pieces 13

3 Jennifer Eccles: gifted and talented but plans on a postcard 19

4 The ambitious fast-tracker 25

5 Eleanor Rigby: rings on her fingers and bells on her toes 33

6 The new mentor: a baptism of fire 39

7 The language of life 47

8 Carrie Anne: oh yes I will, oh no I won't 52

9 Not-so-sweet Caroline 59

10 The crowded classroom 66

11 Boys know about foxes 70

Reader and tutor notes 77

Further Reading 101

Introduction

Trainee teachers need support in school from mentors who are qualified to do the job and able to devote time to it.

Professor Sonia Blandford
Canterbury Christ Church University College

Background

Developing as a Secondary School Mentor: A Case Study Approach for Trainee Mentors and their Tutors has evolved from our experiences as professional mentors in secondary schools and as mentor trainers within large initial teacher training (ITT) partnerships, with Higher Education Institutes (HEIs), Designated Recommended Boards (DRBs) for graduate trainees and School Centred Initial Teacher Training (SCITTS). We quickly learned that mentors working with trainee teachers and teachers in the early years of their careers are often faced with challenges that require the exercise of skills not normally developed in the conventional mentor training programmes offered within ITT partnerships or by local education authorities.

We realised that these challenges often have their roots in the area of professional values and practice. In *Qualifying to Teach – Professional Standards for Qualified Teacher Status (DfES/TTA)*, due prominence is given to this area with standard one (Professional Values and Practice) replicating the professional code of the General Teaching Council for England. The challenges mentors face in working with trainees and teachers in the early years of their careers require careful interpretation of this rubric and there seems to be almost endless scope for sharply contrasting perceptions as to the meaning of the eight statements that articulate the standard. For example, Standard 1.5 states: *'They can contribute to, and share responsibly in, the corporate life of schools.'* At first reading, and perhaps without too much reflection, both a trainee teacher and a mentor might nod in total agreement that this is indeed a worthy and appropriate standard to attain for Qualified Teacher Status (QTS). However, like the other statements, it is susceptible to various interpretations that could very easily be a source of personal and professional contention.

We are aware of a trainee whose placement in a school involved a lengthy journey from home each day and was further complicated by the vagaries of the public transport system. The trainee found it largely impractical to attend after-school activities although she made a special effort to attend departmental and parents' meetings during the course of her placement. However, the mentor took the view that she had not met Standard 1.5 in full. The trainee argued that this was an unfair assessment and maintained that she would have the potential to offer more to the school's corporate life were her personal travel circumstances less problematic. As is so often the case, the mentor applied her value system to the assessment in what she thought was a perfectly acceptable professional way, but had not had the opportunity to consider the nature of the evidential base upon which this particular standard ought to be judged. Indeed, it was agreed, in the light of this experience, that school-based mentors in future should have the option to record a range of assessments including the phrase *'insufficient evidence at this stage to confirm or deny the achievement of this standard but this implies no criticism of the trainee.'* We are not claiming that this is a perfect solution in this particular case, but it does illustrate the profound sensitivity and awareness that are required of a mentor and how easily a formerly successful mentoring relationship can be disturbed, even scarred, by an action undertaken in good faith. In an ideal world there would be no scope for misinterpretation of nationally published professional standards. However, our experience of training mentors over many years has reaffirmed our view that mentors have varying expectations of trainees and seek evidence of differing quality and quantity upon which to support their assessment of professional competence. Well-trained mentors are able to communicate their expectations and establish good working relationships with their trainees with negotiated and clear objectives. But best practice and good intent can be undermined when there is a conflict of values, beliefs and perceptions. Mentors are generally skilled and assured in the area of pedagogy, but less so when challenged by the exigencies and vagaries of human behaviour. It is no easy task as a mentor to sustain a professional relationship with a trainee or a teacher in the early years, when deeply held personal views or immature actions undermine the security and solidarity of the relationship. Because the mentor carries a wide portfolio of roles and responsibilities, it is particularly difficult to manage a trainee through a crisis, as there is an unavoidable tension between the roles of, for example, counsellor and assessor. Of course, no mentor is likely to experience all the scenarios offered in these case studies during the course of their working life, but *Developing as a Secondary School Mentor* offers the opportunity to develop additional skills and to clarify the extent of mentoring responsibilities at those times when professionalism is itself under scrutiny and challenged.

Mentoring

We recognise that 'mentor' means different things to different people. There is a rich literature defining and exploring mentoring. It is not our purpose to offer a definitive view, except to say that the multifaceted roles and responsibilities associated with mentoring mean the potential for challenges is extensive.

The table on page 3 is taken from a mentors' handbook and was compiled with the assistance of a group of school-based mentors and college tutors. There is no attempt to prioritise the tasks or the roles but it does provide a useful checklist. An alternative approach in another training school's policy on mentoring is a section entitled 'The process of mentoring' and lists the following stages: planning and preparation, trainee induction, helping the trainee to observe, observing trainees and giving feedback, and collecting evidence.

In the many handbooks and policy statements we have read, it is rare to find commentary on how a mentor should manage challenging moments. It is almost as if the policies and handbooks are predicated on the assumption that the trainee will progress through a series of stages over a predetermined timescale and emerge fully fledged as a qualified teacher. Our concern is with the trainee or the teacher in the early part of their career who does not progress steadily towards pedagogical competence and who, in the worst-case scenario, verges on the brink of failure or suffers a soul-destroying loss of self-esteem, or finds conflict with a school's values and beliefs. It is at these critical moments that hand-books and policies may be found wanting: the mentor who has been trained to manage challenges is most likely to be able to find the appropriate strategies to enable the trainee to work from the problem to a solution. And just as importantly, the mentor is unlikely to be daunted at the prospect of the challenge before them.

The role of the mentor	The tasks of the mentor
Role model	Be observed teaching, organise observation of other experienced teachers
Coach/trainer	Give feedback, lead reviews, evaluate trainee performance and competence, write reports, complete documentation, etc.
Assessor	Observe trainee teaching
Confidant(e)/advisor	Liaise with school management (e.g. CPD co-ordinator; Heads of Department, etc.), devise teaching timetable for trainee
Tutor/critical friend	Co-ordinate whole school ITT/mentoring provision/programme
Protector/negotiator	Liaise with ITT provider (HEIs)
Ambassador	Integrate ITT into whole school improvement plan
Facilitator	Attend mentor training
Motivator	Provide individual tutorials
Counsellor/advisor	Ensure trainee's health and safety

The emphasis placed on the mentor to model good practice reflects the findings of the research we have undertaken with trainee teachers about the expectations they have of their school-based mentors. The activity in Chapter 1 is based on this work and we recom-mend that it is done before the case studies as it invites discussion and reflection about the role and tasks of the mentor, but contrasts mentors' perceptions with those of their charges. We were certainly surprised by our findings when we sampled 40 post-graduate trainee teachers, but subsequent sampling with other populations has confirmed the out-comes. The results are shared and discussed more fully in Chapter 1 and trainee mentors need to return to these on a regular basis as they work through the case studies because effective mentoring does require recognition of mentees' expectations.

The case study approach

Developing as a Secondary School Mentor uses a tried and tested case study methodology to explore many of the complex management issues faced by mentors working in second-ary education. The learning potential of this approach was amply demonstrated to us at an international conference some years ago by a Harvard University professor who took the delegates through a fascinating narrative focusing on the allegations of a tutor's unfair assessment of an undergraduate. We were intrigued to learn that the case study approach was the main teaching and learning strategy adopted within the Master of Business Administration (MBA) programme at the Harvard Business School. One of the key points to emerge was the vulnerability of the tutor because he had received inadequate training in assessment techniques. In this particular case it was his use of oral feedback that had created the conflict. The issues were his choice of language to identify areas of weakness in the student's work and the apparent inconsistencies between the verbal com-mentary and the written appraisal on the actual assignment. This case study generated some fascinating discussion among the delegates. There was a protracted debate about the natural conflict mentors often face as they are required to be both coach and assessor to a student. It was suggested that these roles should be separated and delegated to other staff rather than subsumed under the auspices of one mentor. Others took the view that a skilled mentor should be capable of fulfilling more than one role and that it was a mentor's responsibility to ensure trainees and students appreciated that the role was driven by specific contexts.

Developing as a Secondary School Mentor offers trainee mentors and their tutors the opportunity to experience mentoring challenges and problems in a safe learning environment. Each case study is derived from our extensive experience as mentors and mentor trainers. The book has a particular focus on mentoring trainee teachers and those in their early years and is cross-referenced, where appropriate, to the standards for qualified teacher status. However, mentors working in different contexts could use the case studies to develop their competence and confidence: the underlying concept is of the mentor as a manager of others' learning. The objective is for mentors to enhance both the individual and the organisation's performance.

The case studies have been trialled with practising mentors and the approach has proved both popular and powerful as a learning style. Although the book can be used by the individual mentor as a self-study resource, by far its most effective deployment is in group activity with a mentor-tutor leading participants through a case study. Each case study represents two hours of interactive learning and is designed to develop trainee mentors' skills in:

- solution-focused approaches to problems;
- managing situations that challenge their professional expertise and competence;
- recognising the significance of the affective domain;
- learning from others' perceptions and analyses.

For mentor trainers to use these case studies effectively, they will need to deploy these skills effectively:

- the management of focused discussion and reflection;
- the ability to summarise and identify key learning points;
- the willingness to clarify purposes and ambiguities;
- the maintenance of engagement through use of encouragement, timing and openness to different ideas and suggestions.

Using the book

After the first chapter, which explores the mentor-mentee relationship and shares some of our research, the first section of the book presents case studies in a format that enables the mentor tutor and participants to move through each episode in the narrative in a structured manner, pausing at key moments to reflect, discuss and decide on appropriate mentoring actions. The second section of the book offers detailed advisory notes to the mentor-tutor on how to manage the learning and highlights the key aspects of mentoring roles and responsibilities. These notes also debate some of the contentious issues that emerge as participants begin to exercise critical judgements of the characters in the narratives. Tutors and individual readers are prompted by a series of questions to consider important issues. These are intended to encourage professional reflection.

The case studies may be considered in any order. The book has been designed so that readers can adapt its contents to their needs or to the priorities of those who are training to become mentors. Ideally, the case studies can be integrated into a mentor training programme as a complement to other course content. However, a case study can be used as a free-standing unit in its own right. For example, a subject department in a secondary school might work through a case study under the guidance of the Head of Department or perhaps a senior manager. This could be a powerful and engaging alternative to a conventional twilight INSET and focus the staff on a professional concern and lead to an agreed departmental action plan for improved professional practice. ITT providers might choose to use some of the case studies in their mentor training programmes to raise awareness and encourage agreed understandings across the partnership: this would not only contribute to the mentors' skill development but also represent a significant exercise in assuring the quality of mentoring offered to trainee teachers. Working through all the case studies would constitute a considerable professional commitment and could be the basis for a written evaluation as part of a course leading to accreditation at post-graduate level.

Developing mentoring skills

It is important to appreciate that the case studies are not examples of perfect solutions. They are based on real experiences and the narratives often have unsatisfactory and unhappy endings. The learning experience is derived from the privilege of being a spectator and having the time, and the interaction with others, to see beyond the immediate challenge. Good mentors, like good teachers, are able to step back from the hustle and bustle of the present and the intensity of interpersonal relationships, to see the bigger picture and to envisage solutions. It is not the book's intention to replicate all the challenges that a mentor may encounter, but to develop a range of skills that enhance a mentor's ability to manage challenges that are unique to their contexts.

As trainers and trainees engage with the case studies, it will be intriguing to note how competing perspectives assert themselves. In using the case studies with different groups we found it was not uncommon for trainee mentors to identify with particular characters in the narratives and almost adopt their personas, whereas others became defensive or aggressive advocates for a particular course of action. Others distanced themselves completely and seemed at ease with a clinical analysis of principles and practice. All these stances are perfectly reasonable and predictable. In sharing them and reflecting upon them real learning takes place. Mentors need to empathise, of course, but must maintain professional discourse and relationships informed by thorough analysis and strategic thinking. In trialling these case studies, we have often been surprised at the polarisation of viewpoints expressed by mentors but we have also been greatly encouraged by their readiness to reconsider. The sharpness of the differences and the forcefulness of consensus certainly bring vigour to the learning but mentor trainers need to embrace these dynamics with sufficient impartiality and receptivity to allow the voices to be heard and due reflection to occur.

Each case study opens with a clear statement of the intended learning outcomes and, usually, cross-references to the standards for QTS. Our experience of using the case studies is that these outcomes are frequently achieved. In addition, participants benefit from the opportunity to reflect and discuss with each other. This develops listening skills, for example, and exposes participants to fresh perspectives.

As each case study progresses episodically, the reader is invited to pause and reflect at various points. After each of these, there have to be agreed next steps or an action plan. It is recommended that pair work or small group work is the most effective strategy to secure good discussion and planning. It is also strongly recommended that the action plan is recorded, shared and displayed in some way. For the reader working through the case study individually, it is vital not to be tempted to read ahead or to glance at the tutor's notes but to have the self-discipline to follow the 'read, reflect and decide' structure.

Many of the case studies include activities to support the process of reflection. For example, in Chapter 3, 'Jennifer Eccles: gifted and talented but plans on a postcard', there is a requirement to draft part of a reference for a trainee teacher who has been called for interview for her first appointment to a neighbouring school. Readers are unlikely to anticipate the sequence of events in each case study and there is no particular merit in predicting the next phase of the narrative. There is merit, however, in thinking about the consequences of actions and anticipating responses to interventions. Well-intentioned actions may be misunderstood and rather than resolving situations can fuel the flames of further disquiet. The importance of the end of case study review is to be able to identify those critical moments where a more skilled mentor might have managed the challenge more effectively. What lessons can be learned? There is a natural tendency, too, to focus on the wellbeing of the trainee teacher/mentee but good mentoring practice is characterised by a mutually beneficial relationship from which both the trainee/mentee and the mentor gain professionally. With the intensity of managing a challenging moment, it is also easy to lose sight of the impact on the quality of teaching and learning and pupils' attainment and achievement. The mentor who fails to manage a challenging moment successfully may well experience strong feelings of disappointment and professional uncertainty. Therefore, in reviewing the case study, the trainee mentor is developing and practising a key skill: professional reflection. When this skill is well formed and embedded, the mentor becomes self-motivated and ultimately capable of reasserting their own self-esteem.

Any parent who has embarked on the challenge of teaching a son or daughter to drive will probably have realised that there is more to success than being able to sit in the passenger seat and offer the benefits of years of driving experience to the nervous teenager behind the wheel. In a similar way, an experienced and successful teacher is not automatically an effective mentor. Sonia Blandford maintains that mentors should be 'qualified to do the job'. We wholeheartedly agree. Of course, there are experienced teachers who have become successful mentors with the minimum of training and without a recognised qualification, but we take the view that high-quality mentoring is at a premium if individuals and organisations are to develop a sustainable culture of professional growth that manifests itself in accelerated pupil learning. An effective mentor is a highly skilled professional with an impressive portfolio of skills, knowledge and understanding. Some people have a natural ability to mentor but the vast majority of practitioners require specific training to achieve full mentor competence. *Developing as a Secondary School Mentor* is not intended to explore every aspect of mentoring. We became increasingly aware during our own training that mentors generally receive a thorough introduction to the role of mentor and guidance on the main principles and practice. There is usually a raft of procedural matters to digest, including paperwork relating to lesson observations and finance. Commonly, mentors are required to organise complementary seminars to support trainees' professional development involving other key personnel within the school. Mentors can usually refer to a handbook for further guidance on several issues, like trainee attendance, assessment and conduct. Some mentors are given guidance on how to deal with those trainees whose performance is falling below expected standards but this tends to focus on the protocols and procedures. Few mentors receive training in the business of managing professional relationships in challenging circumstances where protocols and policies are inadequate to address the interpersonal dimension or indeed anticipate the consequences of highly charged emotions.

Introducing the case studies

The following guide offers a brief outline of the content of each case study. It also identifies the skill area under development and refers to the key sections of the standards for qualified teacher status where appropriate. The case studies involve both trainee teachers and newly qualified teachers (NQTs). Trainees follow different routes to QTS including the Professional Graduate Certificate in Education (PGCE), (BA/BSc/QTS) and the Graduate Training Programme (GTP) and a range of subjects. Mentor trainers are strongly advised to familiarise themselves with the full narrative and the tutor's notes before working the case study with participants. The tutor's notes are particularly important as they suggest procedures, techniques and emphases. They also offer tips and tricks as well as pitfalls to be avoided. Although great stress is laid on the concept of reflective practice, experience has also shown that the pace of delivery is crucial to maintain interest and to compel participants into decision-making. The tutor's notes therefore suggest timings for the management of transitions between episodes and for the related activities.

Chapter 1 What is a mentor?

This is the recommended starter activity that explores trainee teachers' perceptions and expectations of school-based mentors. This is an interactive session with priorities to sort and research findings to compare and contrast.

> **The roles and responsibilities of the mentor: do you know what is expected of you?**

Chapter 2 Picking up the pieces

James has withdrawn from a one-year PGCE course disillusioned by the quality of support he received and has now secured a place on a GTP placement at another school. His mentor needs to deploy a range of strategies to raise his self-esteem and motivation.

> **Do mentors appreciate/value the different routes towards QTS?**

Chapter 3 Jennifer Eccles: gifted and talented but plans on a postcard

Jennifer is an exceptionally talented trainee who has great skill and presence in the classroom but her planning documentation is rather cursory and clearly does not meet the necessary standards.

> **How do mentors weigh the evidence of trainee competence?**
>
> 3.2.1 They make appropriate use of a range of monitoring and assessment strategies to evaluate pupils' progress towards planned learning objectives, and use this information to improve their own planning and teaching.
>
> 3.2.7 They are able to use records as a basis for reporting pupils' attainment and progress orally and in writing, concisely, informatively and accurately for parents, carers, other professionals and pupils.
>
> 3.3.3 They teach clearly structured lessons or sequences of work which interest and motivate pupils.

Chapter 4 The ambitious fast-tracker

David is a mature entrant into the profession, whose commercial background causes friction as he disregards the conventions and protocols that operate within a school.

> **How does a mentor encourage a trainee to rethink the values that he has brought from his previous employment and that he applies to his work in school with unfortunate consequences?**

Chapter 5 Eleanor Rigby: rings on her fingers and bells on her toes

Eleanor clashes with the school ethos as her penchant for jewellery incurs the disapproval of her mentor and the church school's code of dress.

> **How does a mentor manage the conflict in a trainee that clashes with the unwritten conventions within a school?**
>
> 1.3 They demonstrate and promote positive values, attitudes and behaviour that they expect from pupils.

Chapter 6 The new mentor: a baptism of fire

Jeremy has made an immediate impact upon the school as he begins his teaching career after service as a commissioned officer in the army. He is, however, becoming an unwelcome voice in the staffroom where his acerbic remarks and open criticism of staff are ruffling a few feathers. He is most effective when working with older able pupils.

How does the mentor secure self-evaluation and reflection in a NQT who has a strong sense of their own capabilities?

Chapter 7 The language of life

Peter Baggley is a mature entrant to the teaching profession. In his first year of teaching he has a major confrontation with a notoriously difficult Year 11 pupil. Peter feels that the best way to deal with the situation is to speak to the boy's parents on a man-to-man basis but the school wants to avoid his direct intervention at all costs. The mentor is challenged to assist Peter but has to respect the headteacher's directives.

How does a mentor sustain a professional relationship with an NQT who has 'overstepped the mark in a moment of madness'?

1.4 They can communicate sensitively, and effectively, with parents and carers, recognising their roles in pupils' learning and their rights, responsibilities and interests in this.

1.8 They are aware of, and work within, the statutory frameworks relating to teachers' responsibilities.

2.7 They know a range of strategies to promote good behaviour and establish a purposeful working environment.

Chapter 8 Carrie Anne: Oh yes I will, oh no I won't

Carrie Anne is a successful ICT trainee who has no problem in securing her first appointment. However, she reneges on her verbal acceptance of a post and this causes considerable friction between her, the host school that provided a reference, her university and an angry headteacher.

Where do mentors' responsibilities end?

1 Professional Values and Practice: those awarded QTS must understand and uphold the professional code of the General Teaching Council for England.

Chapter 9 Not-so-sweet Caroline

Caroline is an established member of the school's Senior Leadership Team who has recently added the role of professional mentor to her portfolio. The style and nature of her verbal feedback after lesson observations causes disquiet and the trainee teacher complains to his university tutor who does not relish raising this issue.

Who manages the mentor?

Who ensures that the partnership between the school and the college is conducted for the maximum professional development of the trainee?

Chapter 10 The crowded classroom

Anisha, in the final year of her BA/QTS course, raises concerns about the professionalism of the support staff working with her.

> **How does a mentor mediate between paraprofessionals and a trainee?**
>
> 1.6 They understand the contribution that support staff and other professionals make to teaching and learning.
>
> 3.1.4 They take part in and contribute to teaching teams as appropriate in the school. Where applicable, they plan for the deployment of additional adults who support pupils' learning.

Chapter 11 Boys know about foxes

A trainee observes a lesson taught by the deputy head and eventually raises with his mentor some concerns about the treatment of girls and slow learners he has witnessed.

> **How does a mentor ensure the trainee receives appropriate support from working with other professionals?**
>
> 1.2 They treat pupils consistently, with respect and consideration and are concerned for their development as learners.
>
> 1.3 They demonstrate and promote positive values, attitudes and behaviour that they expect from pupils.

The authors

Alan Child and Steve Merrill have been involved in initial teacher training for the last 15 years. Both have managed ITT programmes as Professional Mentors in large comprehensive schools. Over the last three years they have been involved in researching and writing about teacher training with a particular focus on the mentoring role. They have led training sessions on mentoring in schools, colleges and other ITT providers, as well as presenting research papers at national and international conferences. Their work has been published in academic and professional journals but *Developing as a Secondary School Mentor* is their first book.

Note to the tutor

You many wish to photocopy and distribute some of the resources to your trainees. To facilitate this, these resources may also be found on the Learning Matters website – go to www.learningmatters.co.uk/education/secondarymentors.html

1   What is a mentor?

We strongly recommend that the exercise on the role of the mentor in this chapter is undertaken to establish the perceptions of trainee mentors and to share with them the perceptions and expectations of those they mentor. The term mentor has rightly been distinguished from that of coach but is still a title that encompasses a variety of roles and is often a carelessly attributed title to managers and tutors in organisations with no precise definition or job description attached to it. In schools, mentors are often appointed with little formal training but it is assumed that, as successful practitioners, they are capable of fulfilling this demanding role with trainee teachers and those in their early years.

We have explored trainee teachers' and newly qualified teachers' expectations of school-based mentors on several occasions and the emerging consensus provides some important guidelines upon which to build the mentor's credibility and suggests a framework for the skills that underpin successful mentoring.

The attributes of a mentor

The table on page 12 lists the attributes of the secondary school mentor that various groups of trainee teachers identified as pre-requisites for them to feel that their mentor was sufficiently skilled and sensitive to meet their needs as they pursued Qualified Teacher Status. The table can be used in several ways to stimulate reflection and discussion. There is no particular merit in any single approach and trainers may wish to use more than one. Ideally, the programme suggested should be followed to achieve maximum learning.

Approach 1

Offer the table of 18 attributes and invite additional contributions/deletions/amendments. Discussion can be structured in pairs or small groups until there is an agreed amended table.

Approach 2

Offer the table and invite individuals or pairs to attach a level of significance to each attribute. The three categories of significance are *essential*, *desirable* and *highly desirable*.

Approach 3

Having identified the attributes in the two levels of significance, place five of the attributes in a prioritised list that best captures the ideal profile of a secondary school mentor.

Approach 4

Offer the profile below, which represents the findings of research with secondary trainee teachers when asked to identify the three main characteristics of a mentor for whom they had respect and with whom their professional development was likely to progress and invite discussion:

- leads by example;
- possesses specific skills in the mentee's subject area;
- bases judgements on close observation and objective evidence of the mentee's progress.

Approach 5

Offer the table and encourage a scaling activity in which the reader attaches to each attribute a number on the scale of 1 to 5, indicating their sense of their own possession of each attribute.

point 1 = little or none; point 3 = reasonable level; point 5 = secure and well established.

These activities are designed to encourage reflection on the nature of the mentor's role. Although trainee teachers seem to have arrived at a consensus that is predicated on three key attributes, experienced teachers who aspire to the mentor's role will probably want to challenge the consensus and explore the attributes themselves more closely.

'Leads by example', which emerges as the strongest of all mentor attributes, is quite clearly a shorthand term and does an injustice to the thinking and expectations behind it. However, there is obviously an important message here as trainees need to be mentored by a teacher who, to use other clichés, walks the talk or practises what they preach. This in no way undervalues the many other skills the mentor brings to the role but it seems that the relationship between mentor and trainee begins, and is likely to be sustained and successful, where the mentor has high professional credibility. This credibility is probably rooted in classroom pedagogy and practice but extends beyond it.

In the following chapters, the case studies will explore some of these attributes and it might be beneficial to focus on those that relate to some of the points emerging from discussion of this attribute table. For example, in 'The crowded classroom' (Chapter 10) the mentor has to manage a complex situation involving not only her newly qualified teacher but also the support staff working with her as a professional dispute threatens to undermine pupil learning. In 'Jennifer Eccles' (Chapter 3) a highly competent young teacher challenges the perceived wisdom about lesson planning and review.

Attributes of the secondary school mentor

Carries responsibility for pass/fail assessment of trainee	Offers a shoulder to cry on
Conducts regular reviews with mentee	Represents the host organisation's values, principles and practices
Develops his/her own skills through reading and research	Operates as a performance coach
Possesses specific expertise in the mentee's subject area	Monitors mentee's progress at regular intervals
Acts as a trainer	Leads by example
Has counselling skills	Directs mentee towards appropriate professional development opportunities
Has, or is working towards, recognised mentoring qualifications	Bases judgements on close observation and objective evidence of mentee's progress
Acts as a critical friend	Acquires mentoring skills through on the job experience
Assesses mentee's performance against agreed criteria	Manages conflict and issues of professional conduct

2 Picking up the pieces

This case study is particularly relevant to those who have no formal experience of mentoring but who would like to become involved in the process of ITT. It offers an insight into different routes into teaching and an awareness of the needs of the trainees in their early weeks of training. Within this case study trainee mentors will be required to take on a variety of roles in order to appreciate the big picture of working with trainee teachers.

Intended learning outcomes

Do mentors appreciate/value the different routes into teaching?

How do you motivate the trainee who has been disillusioned? There will be opportunities to:

- *understand the importance of providing a meaningful experience for the trainee;*
- *be aware of other routes into teaching apart from the traditional PGCE;*
- *develop skills in motivating the dedicated but disillusioned trainee;*
- *understand why schools engage in initial teacher training;*
- *appreciate the process of selection for trainees.*

Setting the scene

James had completed a degree in religious studies and achieved a 2:1 from a university in his home town. He had always expressed a desire to teach in a secondary school and considered that his natural route into teaching would be to follow a professional graduate certificate of education (PGCE) course at an established higher education institute. In the final year of his degree course he had applied for such a course and impressed the tutors sufficiently to be offered a place. He had thought carefully about his chosen profession, showed a full understanding of the demands of a career in teaching and his subject knowledge was excellent. The tutors who interviewed him were delighted to have him on the course.

After completing his degree James spent three weeks in a local comprehensive school attached to the religious studies department. This convinced him further that he had made the correct decision about his career and he thoroughly enjoyed the experience. The department was also impressed by the contribution that he was able to make to religious studies within the school. He was not only engaged in collaborative teaching but his ICT skills were far superior to those of the department and in the time after the Year 11 pupils had stood down, he was able to contribute to training in this area within the department. He left the school at the end of the summer term feeling confident about his forthcoming course and satisfied with the contribution that he had made in the previous three weeks.

At the beginning of the course in the following September James quickly established himself as an intelligent student who, apart from his own subject knowledge, taught with panache and was quick to understand the theoretical aspects of pedagogy that formed the main part of the first month of the course. For his first practice he had been allocated to a rural comprehensive school that had an excellent reputation as a partnership school with the HEI. He was delighted by this and eagerly awaited his first visit to the school.

He arrived there having forwarded his curriculum vitae as instructed by the college. He had not received a reply from the school, but he was not unduly concerned about this as many of his fellow students were in the same position. After all, this school did have an excellent reputation for its work with trainees. However, on his arrival things began to change. He reported to reception and despite the helpful secretary, one hour later he was still sitting there. Eventually, the head of religious studies appeared, somewhat flustered, saying that the school was not expecting a trainee that day. However, James could stay and observe lessons. The day was spent sitting at the back of classrooms; in some cases with teachers who were not expecting him and who had no idea who he was.

Task one

In order for partnerships to be successful there has to be an established routine for trainees when they arrive at your school. As professional mentors you have overall responsibility for the partnership. Devise an Induction Day Programme for trainees on the first day of their practice. You may like to consider the following.

- *As a trainee, what would you like to know about the school?*
- *Who else from the school should be able to make a worthwhile contribution to the day?*

There is a copy of a sample Induction Day Programme in the reader and tutor notes that may be helpful. Trainee mentors may wish to comment on this programme and compare it with what they have produced in Task One.

Later on day one

James leaves the school at 3.30 p.m. He has been given no indication about what he should do the following day or where to report to. From his experience in the summer he knows that schools are busy and sometimes chaotic places. He believes that things will get better and he is looking forward to getting into the classroom.

For James the remainder of the week is no better: each day resembles the first day and there appears to be no structure to his practice. The following week he consults his college tutor who contacts the school. The school explains that there have been changes in personnel but they are about to appoint a new professional mentor internally and things should improve.

Week three of the practice

James is now disillusioned: he has not done any collaborative planning, a professional mentor has not been appointed and therefore there have been no generic courses provided by the school. His tutor at college merely reiterates that the school has a good reputation for trainees, something with which James would not concur. He realises from conversations with other trainees that he is not progressing. James considers that he has no alternative but to leave the course, despite extensive counselling from his college tutors.

- *Decide what you consider to be the initial responsibilities of the professional mentor, both externally with the HEI and internally with the subject areas in the school.*
- *How did James's first placement school fail him?*
- *How could James's school have been more proactive in ensuring his development in the first month of his practice?*

The future

James feels that he is a failure. After six months of menial jobs he still wants to teach but does not want to repeat the experiences of his PGCE course. He hears about the GTP from a friend and decides to make an application to his local Designated Recommending Body (DRB). He realises that his withdrawal from a PGCE course may be a handicap to his application but nevertheless decides to apply. He also approaches the local comprehensive school where he spent three weeks the previous summer term. They are prepared to accept him, with certain reservations, as a trainee under this programme which will involve on-the-job training. They have never had a trainee before and therefore there is no trained subject mentor in the department. However, the school does have a tradition of well-developed ITT partnerships in other subject areas, and a highly experienced and efficient professional mentor.

You are the professional mentor at the school that is prepared to sponsor James. You attend a meeting with the religious studies department where they put forward their proposals to take James as a graduate trainee. Consider the advantages and disadvantages of such a move. How will the school/department benefit from having a trainee? What caveats would you draw to their attention, particularly bearing in mind that James has had an unfortunate experience in his previous attempt to undertake teacher training?

Advantages that a trainee brings to a school	Disadvantages that a trainee brings to a school

After the meeting a decision is made to support James in his application for the GTP. It is agreed that the religious studies second in department will act as his subject mentor and she will undergo training provided by the DRB. The head of religious studies has been asked to provide a reference for James based on his knowledge of him and his potential to become a successful teacher.

The interview

James must still attend an interview with the DRB, despite the fact that the school has offered him a place to train.

Task four

Devise a suitable interview procedure to decide if James is a viable candidate for the GTP. Your interview should aim to explore the following points that are relevant to selection:

- *James's commitment to teaching;*
- *his potential to achieve the competencies associated with QTS;*
- *reasons why James failed to complete the PGCE course.*

Success

James impresses the representative of the DRB. He is accepted on the course and begins his placement in the religious studies department at the start of the Easter term. (GTP trainees are eligible to begin their training at the start of any term.)

A fresh start

James begins his practice at your school. His induction is relatively easy as he already has an awareness of the procedures that exist in the school from the three weeks that he previously spent there. You, as professional mentor, will need to work closely with the new inexperienced subject mentor. You also realise that James may still be somewhat disillusioned and cautionary about teaching after his experiences on the PGCE. James clearly needs to be motivated and his confidence restored: as professional mentor you will need to establish a meaningful and appropriate programme for James in his first few weeks and this will be achieved with the co-operation of the subject mentor.

Task five

For the purpose of this task you will take on the role of subject mentor. What proportion of James's teaching timetable should be drawn from each member of the RS department? Consider the professional and personal characteristics of the staff and offer your suggestions in percentages, giving a short statement to support your allocation in each case.

Departmental member	Characteristics
Mr Smith	Mr Smith is Head of Department. Although he has only been teaching for six years he is highly experienced, having taught in two schools and also been Head of Year before taking on the post of Head of Department. He was a mature entrant to the profession and he has awareness of the GTP programme as his wife completed it two years ago. He teaches across the age and ability range and is an extremely capable classroom practitioner who is determined to pursue his career in senior leadership.
Mr Jones	Mr Jones is an experienced teacher of some 25 years. He has never had ambitions to rise above being a main professional grade teacher. He may be described, in a critical sense, as being somewhat professionally stagnated. Lessons are generally unimaginative and repetitive from previous years.
Mrs Brown	Mrs Brown has been teaching for four years and is a dedicated practitioner with a wide repertoire of methodology in her lessons. In the recent OFSTED inspection her lessons received particular mention for their variety and interest. She is second in department and has taken on the role of James's subject mentor.
Miss Bradshaw	Miss Bradshaw is an NQT who has settled in well and is contributing to the department in a number of ways. She achieved QTS by following the PGCE course at the college from which James withdrew.
Mr Hobson	Mr Hobson is the assistant headteacher and although not an RS specialist he teaches a 25 per cent timetable with lower school RS classes. He is a strict disciplinarian but liked by the pupils for his sense of humour. He is particularly competent with low-ability groups.

Week six – James flies solo

James has continued to contribute to the department and integrated well. Your decision to attach him to Mr Jones for two classes per week has proved inspirational. Mr Jones is re-energised and the presence of a trainee observing his lessons has resulted in his reflecting and analysing his own practice to the extent that he is now more involved in discussion and debate on learning and teaching. Miss Bradshaw has enjoyed the responsibility of working with James in an informal manner and advising him on the needs and nature of professional assignments required by the DRB. Mr Hobson, despite his questionable subject knowledge, has provided valuable lessons in behaviour management. You are delighted with your first experience of mentoring. James has progressed and is a valued departmental member. Staff within the department have all contributed in their own specific ways and professional development within religious studies has benefited from the presence of James in terms of reflective practice and discussion.

It is now time for James to teach alone as you feel confident that he has the skills to test his own confidence. However, before you allow this you need to discuss lesson planning with James. You are determined that James will succeed and before the lesson with a Year 7 group you arrange to meet James to discuss the content of the lesson.

Task six

Study James' lesson plan on page 18. Consider whether it contains the following:

- *what the pupils should learn (the objectives);*
- *how the pupils will progress (the outcomes);*
- *opportunities and strategies for assessing the learning outcomes.*

What suggestions for improvement would you make?

Lesson plan

Class: Year 7   **Teacher: James**   **Ability: Top set**   **Number of pupils: 25**

Learning objectives:	Learning outcomes:
To know the meaning of the terms theist, atheist and agnostic; To know the factors that influence people's beliefs; To understand the difference between faith and fact.	All pupils will be aware of different belief systems. There will be an understanding of why people have specific views with regard to the existence of God.

Resources/Health and Safety issues:	Key words:
Worksheets, textbooks, interactive whiteboard; Classroom environment.	Faith, evidence, theist, atheist, agnostic

---

Introduction:	Developmental activities:
Starter activity: Why do people believe/disbelieve in God? 3 reasons for each. Share ideas with whole class.	Introduce the words theist, atheist and agnostic to fit in with findings from starter activity. Pupils to write up results of discussions. Group work to share further ideas through discussion.

Plenary:	Pupils with SEN, EAL, G&T/Cross curricular links:
Each group to report back through spokesperson on their findings.	Citizenship: tolerance of people's beliefs. 3 gifted and talented pupils in class.

Evaluation:

You are satisfied, after your suggestions, that James is ready to go ahead with the lesson. You arrange to meet James after school. As he enters your room his expression displays his total satisfaction. Ecstatic would not be an exaggeration. The feedback that James gives you is enthusiastic and at the same time realistic. He reflects upon his lesson professionally and is already considering ways he can improve upon it when he teaches the lesson later in the week. You quietly consider the joys of mentoring and a job well done.

End piece

James continues to progress and his presence brings vitality to the department. He passes his course with distinction and is awarded QTS just over a year after withdrawing disillusioned from a PGCE course. Mr Jones decided that despite James' influence on his teaching it was time to go and took early retirement. James applied for his post at the school and was appointed.

3 Jennifer Eccles: gifted and talented but plans on a postcard

Intended learning outcomes

The trainee mentor will explore the balance between a teacher's classroom competence and the quality of the written documentation that supports practice and evaluate the weighting that is attached to these criteria in the assessment of QTS.

Jennifer is a trainee teacher in her second school placement of a one-year PGCE (Secondary, English). Her first placement school assessed her as an exceptionally talented classroom practitioner, striking excellent relationships with pupils of all ages and abilities. She is very confident and was at ease working with a demanding Year 10 group for whom she developed a fascinating media studies module on TV soaps that really engaged the pupils and led to some excellent work to include in their GCSE coursework folders.

A cautionary note did record, however, that her teaching practice file was poorly organised. More importantly, her lesson plans were rather brief (indeed, there was an unconfirmed suspicion that many were actually written after the lesson). Her lesson evaluations were also rather cursory. Typically, she would enthuse about the classroom atmosphere and her natural self-confidence led her to conclude that the lessons were invariably successful. Jennifer negotiated the following targets for her continuing progression towards QTS with her first placement school mentor:

- to ensure that lesson plans are written on the agreed pro-formas and that all relevant sections are completed;
- to ensure that all taught lessons are evaluated and that subsequent planning is informed by this professional reflection.

In the final paragraph of the first placement report the mentor concluded:

> 'Jennifer Eccles has outstanding potential as a teacher. Her imaginative approaches to teaching and learning, her enthusiasm and her gift of striking positive relationships with staff and pupils are remarkable.'

Jennifer joins her second placement school and presents her subject mentor with a considerable mentoring challenge.

Week two: second placement

Jennifer has settled in well and she has lived up to the positive recommendations received from her first placement school. Quite rightly the mentor has focused on lesson planning. The mentor is concerned about the need for documentation to demonstrate appropriate pedagogy and practice but is not really anticipating any concerns relating to lesson content or teaching and learning styles, as initial and informal visits to Jennifer's classrooms are most encouraging.

Task one

At the end of the second week the mentor asks to see Jennifer's teaching practice file.

Look at the lesson plan and its evaluation, which are representative of the general quality of Jennifer's documentation.

- *Is the documentation at the required standard?*
- *What amendments, additions, deletions would be appropriate?*
- *Attach your comments to the response section of the lesson plan.*

Lesson plan

Teacher: Jennifer Eccles Class: Year 7 Set 1 English Lesson 3 (45 minutes) Number of pupils: 30 (18 boys, 12 girls NC level 4+)

Learning objectives

- to engage pupils in creative writing of poetry (haiku).

Learning outcomes

- Pupils will understand the structure of haiku.
- Pupils will write their own haiku.
- Pupils will appreciate the process of selecting key emotive words.

Outline/Timings of lesson

Introduction/starter: take register, return books with marked homework; issue merits for good work
Read examples of successful writing of limericks
Main body:
Issue stimulus material (A4 sheet containing six haiku)
Explore poems, discover structure; identify key words. (Might use some drama techniques like tableau to aid comprehension)
Pupil task: to write their own haiku on the theme of age but JE to write one with them on the whiteboard and to share thinking process (shared writing)
Plenary: Share examples of good writing; reinforce haiku structure and set homework (haiku sequence)

Additional notes: Don't forget to print large font copy for Maria. Check on missing homework.

Evaluation: this lesson went really well. The pupils produced some great haiku and really grasped the idea of making every word count and looking at small details to make a big point. They are a great class to teach so enthusiastic and willing and they seem to like me and what I do.

Observations on Jennifer's lesson plan

Week four: second placement

Jennifer has continued to teach effectively. Her reaction to the mentor's review of her teaching practice file was encouraging. She seemed appreciative of the advice and the reasons behind the emphasis on the importance of record keeping. However, there has been less progress than her mentor hoped. Her learning objectives are clearer and she does give more information about the activities she has planned but her evaluations still seem rather superficial and do not focus sharply enough upon learning outcomes.

The mentor is beginning to think that Jennifer is so self-assured, anticipating her successful completion of the PGCE, that she is not giving due consideration to the issues her mentors have raised. The mentor also thinks that she can probably have a successful placement but experience tells her that teaching virtually full time in the induction year is rather different from the reduced loading of the PGCE. The mentor wants Jennifer to learn that good planning is about teacher survival as well as ensuring pupil learning.

The mentor receives a request from a neighbouring school for a reference for Jennifer, who has been shortlisted for interview. Jennifer is really excited about this as the school has just gained Performing Arts College status and she desperately wants to secure a job that offers the possibility of sixth-form teaching.

Week six: second placement

Jennifer is unsuccessful in her interview and is extremely disappointed. The post was offered to a temporary contract holder at the school who had more experience. The head-teacher offers her very complimentary feedback that is promising for the future. He hints that there may well be a one-year contract available in English to cover a maternity leave and makes it absolutely clear that Jennifer would be a strong candidate. However, he raises a concern about her application that relates to lesson planning and evaluation and advises her to strengthen this area if she re-applies to his school and certainly in other applications. This remark causes Jennifer some consternation and she raises it with the mentor at her next tutorial. She has concluded that something in her reference has highlighted this area of concern about her work. She wants to see her reference because she believes that it has been overly influential in the failure of her recent application.

Task three

References are privileged documents and Jennifer has no right to see what was written about her in confidence.

You may be disappointed that the headteacher in the neighbouring school has flagged up this concern. However, he has not broken any protocols of confidentiality because he has not revealed the contents of the reference you submitted.

What do you do now?

Do you stand your ground and say that a reference is a confidential document and you cannot show it to her?

Do you reiterate your concern about lesson planning but reaffirm her many other excellent teacher qualities and her promising future?

Do you offer additional support in lesson planning and evaluation so that her skills are developed and you can anticipate writing an even more supportive report in the future?

Do you suggest that she has in fact jumped to conclusions and that your reference was not likely to undermine her chances? Will you suggest that the head teacher actually gained his impression from her interview responses?

Do you show her the reference to put her mind at ease?

Week eight: sting in the tail

The last tutorial was successful. Jennifer has begun to offer excellent lesson plan documentation and her evaluations are far more professional and reflective. She has secured an appointment for September in an LEA that is offering several incentives to attract NQTs.

On Jennifer's last day in school, she is given a fond farewell with a gift from the English department staff and several of her classes. In her short speech of thanks she is quite emotional and compliments the school for its professionalism in supporting her during her teaching practice. The mentor is personally mentioned and thanked.

End piece

On leaving the staffroom, the mentor makes one final check of her pigeon-hole and sees a bright blue envelope. This is a thank you card from Jennifer but it contains the following text:

Dear_____

This card is a token of my appreciation for your help and support during my eight weeks at _____ High School. I could not leave without sharing with you some of the things that have been in my mind ever since I failed to get the job at _____ High School.

I know that you needed more evidence of my lesson planning and that you thought I did not put enough detail into my teaching practice file. You said on several occasions that your assessment of me against the standards for QTS had to be based not only on lesson observations but also on the completed lesson plan pro-formas and on my lesson evaluations.

I remember you showing me the Handbook of Guidance that said, 'the main source of evidence will be trainees' lesson plans and their teaching'. What I still find difficult is the balance between the planning documentation and the actual lesson itself. Surely you could see from my performance in the class that I was planning and thinking well? I did not want to over-script my lessons otherwise I would have become dull and prescriptive. Aren't imagination and spontaneity the things that really matter? As my grandmother used to say: the proof of the pudding is in the eating.

With best wishes,
Jennifer Eccles

Task four

Some mentors might feel moved to reply to Jennifer's letter. Some might be so offended that they contemplate recourse to a formal complaint. Your task is to prepare a response to the following question:

How does a mentor balance the quality of lesson planning documentation against the quality of lesson delivery?

Here are some prompts to guide your thinking:

- *Well-planned lessons with clear learning objectives and learning outcomes that meet the requirements of the school's scheme of work/National Curriculum and that demonstrate an awareness of assessment for learning are to be encouraged and welcomed as part of a trainee's portfolio.*
- *You may argue that high-quality planning is the heart of successful pedagogy. But how detailed do you expect these lesson plans to be?*
- *If the plans are not well implemented in the classroom, the trainee is probably not progressing towards QTS. If the trainee is at ease in the classroom and building good and effective relationships with the pupils, and there is solid evidence of pupil learning because of the teacher's actions, is this more persuasive evidence of progress towards QTS even if the planning is less thorough?*
- *Should a trainee adopt lesson planning systems as advised by the ITT provider or the school? Is lesson planning standardised in the school? Would trainees in different departments find different expectations placed upon them and could this raise issues of quality control in assessing progress towards QTS and Standards 3.1.1 and 3.1.2?*

4 The ambitious fast-tracker

Intended learning outcomes

This case study will examine the role of the mentor in managing the over confident fast-track trainee in meeting the following crucial standards for QTS:

1.3 Trainees demonstrate and promote positive values, attitudes and behaviour that they expect from pupils.

1.5 Trainees can contribute to and share responsibility in the corporate life of the school.

1.6 Trainees understand the contribution that other professionals make to teaching and learning.

1.7 Trainees are able to improve their own teaching, by evaluating it, learning from the effective practice of others and from evidence. Trainees are motivated and able to take increasing responsibility for their own professional development.

3.1.4 Trainees take part in and contribute to teaching teams as appropriate in the school.

Furthermore, the mentor will be required to address issues of confidentiality.

Setting the scene

The fast-track programme was launched in 2000 as part of a drive to modernise the teaching profession in England. The programme is about identifying future leaders in education and providing them with training, support, experience and the opportunity to achieve their potential. The fast-track selection process is demanding and is designed to test the suitability of candidates to the limit. If it sounds daunting it is because the fast-track teacher would relish such a challenge. The accelerated development programme steers people towards leadership positions in schools and is for those who have a strong academic record and are able to complete a rigorous selection and assessment procedure and secure a place on a PGCE course. Fast-track trainees have access to a wealth of high-quality professional development opportunities and resources.

Current fast-trackers who receive these benefits and enhanced starting salaries report a degree of cynicism and hostility towards them both from fellow trainees and established staff within schools. It is this hostility and cynicism that will be the basis of this case study. As it unfolds, your skills as a mentor will be tested as David provides you with a number of challenges.

David is a mature entrant to the profession having run his own computer software company for a number of years. He is in his mid-thirties. He has joined the fast-track scheme and is completing a PGCE (ICT and business studies) at your partnership HEI. He arrives at your school for his first practice. David looks professional and conveys an air of confidence. The other trainees seem in awe of him and during introductions in your induction meeting he confidently assures you, and the other trainees, that in five years' time he will be a headteacher in a failing school and turning it around. Your own school is not going to provide him with the opportunity to test his skills in this area. It is a highly successful large 11–18 comprehensive and to some extent traditional, with an established staff whose age profile is skewed towards 45+. Because of this traditionalism the school enjoys an enviable reputation in the middle-class area that it serves.

Task one

As professional mentor you receive a telephone call from David's tutor at the college. David has complained to his tutor that he has not been given sufficient space at the work stations in the departmental office and consequently feels that he is not being given equality in terms of his professionalism and, in particular, as a fast-track trainee. As professional mentor you are somewhat surprised by this. The ICT and business studies department is extremely experienced in initial teacher training and enjoys an excellent reputation and first-class relationships with the college.

As professional mentor you have to deal with this communication from the college. How will you do it? You may like to consider the following points:

- *your reaction to the college tutor;*
- *your approach to the subject mentor and the department;*
- *your subsequent conversation with David.*

As professional mentor you have overall managerial responsibility for the management of the partnership. In your discussions about this challenge you should consider where your priorities lie in terms of the college, the trainee and the department.

The results of your decisions

The college tutor is new to his post and has, in the weeks before the practice, been somewhat intimidated by David. You point out to him that you are not prepared to be dictated to in this way and that David is a guest in your school. Although he is following the fast-track scheme he must be prepared to accept what the school is able to provide. You realise that there are certain extras that you need to provide for those involved in fast-track but these are of a management nature and you feel that David's complaint is unjustified and unreasonable. You point out the experience of the department in ITT and their past successful record in this area. You make the tutor aware that you will not inform the fast-track co-ordinator in order that David is given a chance to succeed in the school.

You relay the nature of the conversation with the college tutor to the subject mentor and the department. Their first reaction is astonishment followed by anger. After calming them down you assure them of your full support and the fact that David will be left in no uncertain terms as to what is required of him if he is to complete his practice at the school successfully.

You decide to see David alone. (As professional mMentor you may like to consider whether this was the most appropriate action or whether you should have been accompanied – possibly by the subject mentor or a colleague from the senior leadership team.) David is amazed that his contact with the tutor should have caused so much disquiet within the school. He points out that when he was in business he was used to going to the top if he had a problem and he viewed the tutor as his advocate in this situation. Furthermore, he claimed that he had established a good working relationship with the tutor who fully understood his potential as a future school leader and the contribution that he would make to the teaching profession.

Consider how you would reply to David as a result of his refusal to accept that there had been a lack of protocol in his actions. You may like to consider the following points in terms of the mentor's role and tasks:

protector/negotiator	liaise with ITT provider (HEIs)

The following QTS standards are also appropriate to the discussion and a view from David as to how these may now be implemented is relevant:

1.5 Trainees can contribute to and share responsibility in the corporate life of the school. 3.1.4 Trainees take part in and contribute to teaching teams as appropriate in the school.

After prolonged negotiations David accepts that he has acted hastily and agrees that in future should he have any concerns he will approach the school (either through the subject mentor or, if necessary, the professional mentor).

After these initial problems, David seems to accept that he has much to learn in terms of the way that schools are organised, and although many of his previous managerial skills are transferable he realises that he has a lot to learn from his school experience. As professional mentor, in addition to providing the general professional studies course for all trainees, you are required to provide an insight into aspects of school management for fast-track trainees.

Task two

You must devise a specialised course for a fast-track trainee that will provide experience of school management issues. It will be helpful if you complete the table below.

Management issue	How the issue will be addressed

Suggestions to help with this task are given in 'Reader and tutor notes'.

Week two: David is involved in collaborative planning

After two weeks of observation and involvement in the in-house fast-track programme David becomes involved in collaborative planning. He meets the subject mentor to plan a lesson for a Year 9 top ability class. The subject mentor asks David to provide a detailed lesson plan as a basis for the discussion. He produces the plan for the subject mentor on the day before the meeting.

Lesson plan

Class: Year 9	Teacher: David	Ability: Top set	Number of pupils: 25	Subject: ICT

Learning objectives: To get the children to understand how to operate mail merge as an ICT skill	Learning outcomes: Awareness of skills involved in mail merge
Resources/Health and Safety issues: Computers	Key words: Mail merge
Introduction: Teacher explanation of mail merge process	Developmental activities: Pupils to engage in mail merge activity on computers
Plenary: Summarise lesson	Pupils with SEN, EAL, G&T/Cross-curricular links: 3 pupils gifted in maths 2 pupils gifted in English No cross-curricular links
Evaluation:	

The subject mentor comes to see you to express concern at this plan. As professional mentor you share this concern and you decide to be present at the meeting with David and the subject mentor.

Task three

Now prepare for your meeting with David. Knowing him as you do you realise that the meeting may be rather fraught. You need to be fully prepared and may like to consider the following points in your planning.

- *Are both parties clear on the purpose of the meeting?*
- *Identify your concerns about the lesson plan.*
- *How appropriate is it for the professional mentor to be directly involved in what may be described as a subject area matter?*
- *How will you justify the fact that both subject mentor and professional mentor are present at the meeting?*
- *Anticipate David's reaction to your comments about the lesson plan.*
- *How would you ensure that David acts upon your advice to produce a satisfactory outcome to the meeting?*

Trouble within the department

Surprisingly David accepts the points that you make about his lesson plan. It certainly proved helpful to have a model lesson, plan at the meeting. David goes away and redesigns his own plan for the lesson, which is much more detailed and appropriate, with a clear progression from start to finish and realistic and achievable objectives. Both you and the subject mentor are more optimistic, not only about David's planning but also his willingness to listen. David's actual execution of the lesson is also good and it seems that progress is being made at last. However, the calm is short-lived as David continues to challenge.

Within the department David has made no secret of the fact that he is a fast-track trainee and that he has ambitions well beyond staying in the classroom. These references to aspiring management and increased salary cause resentment among a dedicated and able department. The department react to this and show some reluctance to help David in all aspects of his training. Relationships reach a low and the subject mentor turns to you in desperation. The subject mentor does not want to relinquish responsibility, but the feelings of the department are justified. The challenges of supporting a fast-track trainee are proving more demanding than could ever have been anticipated. You share the subject mentor's concerns and also her determination to see the project through. The department have already proved their ability to work with trainees in the past but they have been seriously challenged by David in only his first week at the school.

Task four

You have to work closely with the department in order to convince them that they have a role to play in David's development. You also have to provide support for the subject mentor.

The priority for the professional mentor is to ensure that the subject mentor feels supported and able to complete her role. The role of the professional mentor at challenging times goes beyond a relationship with the trainee alone. In formulating a support programme for the subject mentor who feels threatened or lacks confidence in their ability you should consider the following role/task of the mentor:

Role: Confidante/advisor   *Task: Liaise with school management (e.g. CPD co-ordinator, Heads of Dept, etc.)*

Devise a short-term plan that will be aimed at the following:

- *motivating the subject mentor;*
- *restoring the confidence of the subject mentor;*
- *allowing the subject mentor to mediate and convince the department of the value of persevering with David.*

After working with the subject mentor, it is now necessary to work in conjunction with her and the department. Formulate a plan in which you will meet with the department but allow the subject mentor to take the initiative in the meeting.

▶

> *The professionalism of the department comes into its own. They agree to take on the challenge of David and to educate him about the reality of schools. You see David with the subject mentor and he again promises to conform to the needs of the department and show a degree more humility in his relationships with people in the school.*

David cannot keep his mouth shut

As part of David's experience of management activities in the school you have arranged for him to observe a senior leadership team meeting. You have made two points explicit to David:

- should there be anything contentious at the meeting he may be asked to leave;
- everything that he observes is confidential.

There is nothing contentious at the meeting and David remains throughout. A discussion centres around the time that school should end on the final day of the Christmas term. It is decided that school will finish earlier than originally planned but that this information will not be conveyed to staff or pupils for another week.

In the meantime David attends a year tutors' meeting where the head of the year is asked about arrangements for the final day of term. The head of year does not know the final details but David, with an air of authority, enlightens the meeting that an early finish is planned as he attended a senior leadership team where the decision was made. The year tutor and other members of staff present look on this information provided by a trainee in disbelief. Why is it that a trainee is privy to this information when the rest of the staff are not aware of it? Immediately after the meeting the head of year approaches you and aggressively demands an explanation.

Task five

Clearly David has placed you in an awkward situation. The Head of Year has a point. He explains that staff within his year team feel undervalued because a trainee is aware of and sharing decisions at senior leadership level that the permanent staff do not know about. As professional mentor you have to consider and act on the following questions:

- *How do you appease the Head of Year and his team?*
- *Why was the information regarding the end of term confidential?*
- *What action do you take against David?*

You might like to consult 'Reader and the tutor notes', page 84, which identify possible solutions to the situation.

You manage to convince the head of year and the tutorial team that the senior leadership team decision was not meant to be kept from staff but permission was needed from the governing body before the decision could be ratified. You see David, who is actually contrite on this occasion, and point out the embarrassing situation that he has placed you in. You take the decision to suspend him unofficially for two days in order to give him time to reflect upon his actions. He returns to school and immediately seeks you out. He has written you a letter.

Dear professional mentor

Over the last two days I have had time to reflect not only on my actions in divulging information that I was privy to at the senior leadership team meeting but also on the progress of my practice so far with particular reference to my place on the fast-track scheme.

I realise that my actions in giving information were inappropriate and I am able to fully empathise with the feelings of the Head of Year and his team. I have written a full apology to all concerned at the meeting. I have also reflected upon my attitude to yourself and members of the department over the last few weeks. I realise that both working and managing in a school cannot be equated to the world of business in which I am used to working.

I clearly have much to learn and I assure you that I will adopt a more positive attitude to the remaining time that I am privileged to work in this school.

If you feel that you would like to discuss the contents of this letter with me please do not hesitate.

Yours,
David

The practice draws to a close

You are surprised by the content of the letter and David's acceptance of the consequences. As professional mentor you feel quietly pleased with the result of the decision that you have made. You arrange to meet David and agree that the remainder of the practice will be completed with a clean sheet. David also informs you that he has sent a similar letter to the Head of Department and, after discussions, hopes for a similar new start in that area.

David keeps to his word and the practice is completed. His lesson planning improves and his attitude to staff and pupils is far more acceptable. In the final general professional studies session he formally thanks you for all your work and says how much he has learned and gained from the practice.

Task six

As Professional Mentor it is your final task to write a reference for David for his next practice school. You should refer in particular to the following standards and how David has addressed them.

1.3 Trainees demonstrate and promote positive values, attitudes and behaviour that they expect from pupils.

1.5 Trainees can contribute to and share responsibility in the corporate life of the school.

1.6 Trainees understand the contribution that other professionals make to teaching and learning.

3.1.4 Trainees take part in and contribute to teaching teams as appropriate in the school.

End piece

Your reference for David was positive and highlighted that he had learned a lot from his first practice at your school. You said that he was willing to learn and despite his experience and maturity, realised that there were major differences between schools and the world that he was used to. No direct reference was made to the problems that had been encountered in the first part of the practice.

David completed both the PGCE and the fast-track course. He was appointed to a post in a school in his home town where his experiences in the world of business came to the forefront and he was able to negotiate two further responsibility points than were originally offered.

5   Eleanor Rigby: rings on her fingers and bells on her toes

Intended learning outcomes

In this case study, what seems an incidental and rather irrelevant issue to the main business of developing teaching skills in a young trainee teacher requires the exercise of high-order personal skills to represent and maintain the school's ethos without undermining the trainee's potential as a teacher.

Setting the scene

Eleanor is a trainee teacher in her first placement of a one-year PGCE (secondary English) course at an HEI. For her first school experience, she has been assigned to St Hilda's Church of England High School, a formal comprehensive school of 1500 pupils aged 11–18. The school is well respected in the area and its standard intake of 250 pupils is selected from around 500 applicants each year. Selection procedures are based not on academic ability but on the parents' commitment to the church. A 'reference of faith' from an appropriate minister forms the basis of admittance.

The school prides itself on its pupils' appearance and there is a strict uniform code. As the school is split site, pupils are regularly observed by the public as they transfer between sites and there is a perceived need to maintain standards. The teaching staff at St Hilda's are in sympathy with the Christian ethos of the school and determined to maintain the standards that make it a pleasant place to teach. Along with the uniform standards there is a strict code of behaviour that ensures a well-disciplined and supportive atmosphere.

Eleanor's college has stated that they initially had concerns about whether to accept her on the PGCE course and prior to final acceptance she had to complete a voluntary practice of two weeks in the summer term before the start of the PGCE. She did the placement and the college was satisfied that she met the criteria for completing a course of teacher education.

Eleanor arrives at your school with six other trainees for her first placement after four weeks of theory at the college. You soon realise that Eleanor is going to present you with a considerable mentoring challenge.

As this case study develops you will face a number of events that will test your mentoring skills in deciding whether Eleanor is meeting the following standards:

1.3 They demonstrate and promote positive values, attitudes and behaviour that they expect from pupils.
1.5 They can contribute to and share responsibility in the corporate life of the school.
1.7 They are able to improve their own teaching, by evaluating it, learning from the effective practice of others and from evidence. They are motivated and able to take increasing responsibility for their own professional development.

Denim and gems

The group of trainees has arrived at school and they have been given an early morning cup of coffee in the staff room by the school secretary. They are told that you, as professional mentor, will be along shortly to meet them and to tell them about the induction programme for the day.

In the meantime, one of your subject mentors arrives at your office looking concerned. She tells you that one of the trainees has a pierced nose with a very distinctive ring through it and a similar piece of jewellery through her eyebrow (no form of jewellery is allowed to be worn by pupils at the school). She is wearing denim jeans and a revealing T-shirt.

The subject mentor is clearly concerned by the appearance of this trainee and looks to you to handle the situation.

Task one

As professional mentor you have a duty to maintain the standards of the school and also to preserve the credibility of the trainee. Furthermore, you have a decision to make on whether Eleanor is meeting Standard 1.3.

Decide how you will approach Eleanor.

- *Will Eleanor's appearance affect your relationships within the college?*

- *At this point will you inform the college of Eleanor's appearance or will you rely on your own judgement to solve the problem?*

Day three of the placement

You met Eleanor on the first day and she agreed to conform to the school's dress code. You pointed out the standards that the school expected and that, if Eleanor did not conform, her credibility in the classroom would be adversely affected. On the first day she told you that the body piercings would have to be removed 'professionally' and asked whether you knew of a body piercing shop in the vicinity. After you, as professional mentor, had given an appropriate answer to this question, Eleanor returned to school at lunchtime and you were satisfied with her appearance.

However, the English subject mentor approaches you at the end of day three looking agitated. The English subject mentor is in her first year as a mentor and has been teaching for four years. Despite her relative inexperience you recommended her for the role as it would make a major contribution to her professional development.

The subject mentor explains that she has designed a programme of observation for Eleanor but in her first observation she sat Eleanor at the back of the room and did needlepoint. She made no notes during the lesson despite the fact that the subject mentor had given her guidelines to observe, focusing initially on starters to the lesson and behaviour management techniques.

When approached by the subject mentor Eleanor described her needlepoint as thera-peutic and said that it helped her to concentrate.

The subject mentor is concerned and asks you to intervene in this case.

Task two

You agree to meet Eleanor.

- *How do you set up this meeting?*
- *What is the purpose of this meeting?*
- *What are the outcomes that you would expect from this meeting?*

Day four of the placement

You decide to meet Eleanor alone. At the meeting Eleanor reiterates her belief that needle-point is therapeutic and that is why she had been doing it. You point out that this is not acceptable and that from now on Eleanor must follow the guidelines for observation laid down by the subject mentor.

You also emphasise the ability of the subject mentor and how, as a relatively new teacher, she is able to empathise with the demands of the PGCE course.

You reach agreement with Eleanor that she will follow the observation programme designed by the subject mentor and that this programme has your full support.

You conclude the meeting by telling Eleanor that you would like to see her in a week's time and that you will want to see her observation notes on the following, as defined in the subject mentor's programme:

- how learning objectives are identified within English lessons;
- starter activities to lessons;
- plenary activities in lessons;
- behaviour management techniques in the English department.

Week two of the placement

The time has come for your meeting with Eleanor to discuss her observations of English classes. The subject mentor has made it clear to you in informal meetings that she is far happier with Eleanor's attitude and that, although she has not had access to her lesson observation notes, Eleanor has been far more positive in her verbal comments.

Furthermore, Eleanor has stated an interest in contributing to the corporate life of the school by participating in the lunchtime poetry appreciation society and the after-school debating club.

As professional mentor you are optimistic that progress has been made and that the ini-tial doubts you and the subject mentor had have been dealt with in a professional manner.

However, your optimism is short-lived when you meet Eleanor and read her lesson observation notes (below).

Lesson observation notes

7A2: English – Mr Smith

This bloke hasn't got a clue – he is doing my head in so what is he doing to the kids? They are all just listening and there is no interaction.

7B3: English – Miss Jones

Probably the best lesson so far but still leaves much to be desired. At least the kids are talking. Not sure that they are talking about the lesson though! Needs to have a bit more life in the lesson. I could on the whole do a lot better.

9A1: English – Mrs Brown

Why do they have to concentrate on preparing the kids for SATs? You would think that all that matters is exam results. Little movement around the class.

10B4: English – Mr Jackson

This is the worst lesson I have ever seen. This bloke is useless. He should be doing a PGCE … I am sure he has never done one.

Task three

You are horrified by what you read and you realise that Eleanor has not concentrated on the programme that had been agreed the previous week. You are aware that the English department is one of the strongest in the entire school, a fact confirmed by the OFSTED inspection in the previous academic year. The department is also used as a model of excellence in the LEA and its lesson design and content is always considered an example of good practice.

Nevertheless, you ask Eleanor to explain her remarks. She tries to justify her comments but they are not based on fact. They reflect her own ideas of teaching, which are fundamentally flawed. You decide that the time has come to involve the college tutor. A meeting is arranged.

You need to determine the nature of the meeting and the desired outcomes. Consider the following questions that Eleanor may raise:

- *Am I going to be asked to leave the school/course?*
- *How will my future be affected?*
- *What is going to happen to me at the end of this meeting?*

Prepare for the meeting with the college tutor and answer the questions you think Eleanor might raise.

One day later in week two

The meeting with the college tutor goes well. He is understandably sympathetic to the concerns of the school. Eleanor is given a formal warning about her future conduct. It is agreed that she will now follow the observation programme with the same classes as before.

The school and the college will be looking for far more positive comments on lessons. In this meeting it appears that Eleanor has realised that she has to conform to all the school's requirements.

As professional mentor you agree to do four joint observations and then compare notes. Eleanor sees this as a positive development.

Once again you are optimistic.

Week four: Eleanor goes it alone

Eleanor has participated in a number of collaborative teaching activities. She has been co-operative and has developed relationships with the pupils who seem to enjoy her involvement. The subject mentor now feels that Eleanor has the skills to teach a class alone. The lesson is prepared in collaboration with the subject mentor who is quietly confident that Eleanor will prove a success. The subject mentor is also pleased with the way that Eleanor has developed and is satisfied with her own success as a mentor.

However, at the start of the lesson Eleanor tells the class that they should refer to her by her first name. The subject mentor is not happy with this unexpected development but decides to allow the lesson to continue and make the point during feedback after the lesson.

The lesson content is good and Eleanor shows a very satisfactory level of development at this point in the PGCE programme.

The subject mentor points out the very positive nature of the lesson but when she approaches the fact that Eleanor insisted on the use of her first name and that this is not acceptable Eleanor becomes aggressive towards the subject mentor. She storms out of the meeting.

The subject mentor tells you as professional mentor about this latest development. Your mentoring skills are again being significantly challenged.

Week seven: the practice draws to a close

Eleanor, perhaps surprisingly, completes her last few weeks of the practice successfully and without incident. The visit from her college tutor is positive and in terms of the standards for qualified teaching status it is decided that Eleanor is working at a level higher than expected at this time. The tripartite review with Eleanor, her college tutor and the subject mentor has gone particularly well.

As the practice draws to a close it is time for you to analyse Eleanor's practice as part of your own learning. For the adult learner the following three elements are features of the learning cycle:

- learning is reflective;
- learning is experiential;
- learning is episodical.

Task four

Decide what you, as professional mentor, and your subject mentor have learned from Eleanor's practice, taking into account these elements.

- *How would you change your approach to mentoring from your experience with Eleanor?*

- *How would you expect the subject mentor to change her approach to mentoring?*

You have to write Eleanor's final report. This will act as an informative document for her second practice school.

Your report should concentrate on the following broad headings related to the standards for QTS:

- *professional values and practice;*
- *knowledge and understanding;*
- *teaching.*

End piece

Despite the fact that she had developed at St Hilda's School, Eleanor decided that she was not going to continue with her career in teaching. She did not begin her second practice and withdrew from the PGCE course.

6 The new mentor: a baptism of fire

Intended learning outcomes

This case study develops the mentor's skills in judging the appropriate basis upon which to seek support and advice from other colleagues but also poses the question of the mentor's autonomy and the right to abrogate responsibility at critical moments.

Setting the scene

You have just taken on your new role at Countryside Comprehensive School as mentor to the newly qualified teachers who have been appointed for the new academic year. You are excited by this task. Your own experience, despite the fact that you have only been teaching for seven years, is extensive. This is your second school and as well as being professional mentor you are also head of religious studies and have had two years' previous experience as a head of year. You see the role of professional mentor as important to your own professional development as you look to extend your experience in order to apply for posts at senior leadership level.

Countryside Comprehensive School is an idyllic school to work in. It is an 11–16 school of 800 pupils, situated in a large thriving village of 8500 inhabitants. The school serves the outlying villages in the predominantly rural area. The intake is from the children of high-income workers who generally commute to the two large conurbations within a 30-mile radius. Parental expectations are high and these are reflected in a GCSE success rate of some 80 per cent of pupils achieving 5 GCSEs at A*–C grade and the fact that the school is over-subscribed. The school is a Language College and has DfES Training School status.

This year the school has employed five newly qualified teachers. You feel, as professional mentor, that this is an optimum number both for you to develop your skills and for the NQTs to interact and reflect.

However, for the purposes of this case study we will be concentrating upon one of these newly qualified teachers who will provide you with a number of challenging moments.

Jeremy has been appointed as a new member of the geography department. At 45, he is more mature than the average NQT. However, his background is impressive. Having retired from the army as a lieutenant colonel he completed a one-year PGCE at a local college to achieve QTS. His military record was impressive, having served with distinction as a lieutenant in the Welsh Guards in the Falklands War. Subsequently, he attended Staff College and held a number of prestigious appointments both in this country and abroad. He is an imposing figure and having met him at interview you are somewhat overawed by his appearance and presence. He is clearly a most confident person. Nevertheless, you refuse to be daunted and resolve to manage Jeremy in exactly the same way as you do the other NQTs. From his experience he clearly has a lot to offer the school and your initial thoughts are that as a new professional mentor you will have much to learn from his obvious and proven leadership qualities. However, in his college reference, there is a cautionary note.

'Jeremy clearly has many attributes that will ensure that he makes a positive contribution to the teaching profession. However, in his practice schools, despite his skills in the classroom, he can be somewhat arrogant about his abilities and has in fact criticised practice by experienced teachers at all levels.'

The week before the start of term

During the week before the start of term you organise an induction day. This is an innovation for the school and you feel that it will be beneficial both for you and the NQTs to get to know each other before the pressure of the new term becomes a reality. It becomes apparent at the induction day that Jeremy is determined to communicate his experiences to all the other members of staff involved. Modesty is certainly not one of his attributes.

Task one

Devise an Induction Day programme for the NQTs prior to the start of the term. You may like to consider the following.

- *As an NQT what would you have liked to know before starting your new post?*
- *Who else from the school would be able to make a worthwhile contribution to the day?*
- *How would you balance the formal and the informal aspects of the day?*

Note: You may choose to omit this task if you have worked on the similar task in Chapter 2.

The start of term

At the start of term staff meeting Jeremy continues to display his confident character. He mixes with all staff and lets them all know his past achievements and his future ambitions. Part of the staff meeting allows you time to meet all the new NQTs. At this meeting you give out your first observation programme as it is a statutory requirement that all NQTs are observed in their first three weeks and provided with written feedback. Jeremy will be observed by you in the second week teaching a Year 8 class for geography.

The second week of term: Jeremy's observation

You arrive to observe Jeremy's lesson. As the lesson progresses you make the following observations:

- he arrives 10 minutes late for the lesson;
- the lesson objectives are not clearly conveyed to the pupils;
- there are a number of basic spelling mistakes on the handouts;
- Jeremy's relationship with the class is somewhat 'distant' and the vocabulary that he uses is at times too difficult for the class;

- there is no formal lesson plan available;
- Jeremy's record book is not up-to-date;
- there is no plenary to the lesson.

Clearly you are concerned about what you have seen.

Task two

Prepare the written feedback that you will give Jeremy using the following headings in association with the standards for qualified teacher status in the induction year. Use the Feedback form on page 43:

- *Professional values and practice.*
- *Knowledge and understanding.*
- *Teaching.*

What do you think Jeremy's reaction to your observations will be?

The meeting with Jeremy does not go well. He asserts that the 'niceties' of lesson plans, objectives and plenaries are only appropriate to trainees and not practising teachers – which he now is.

Decide how you will reply to Jeremy in the light of his assertions. You may like to consider the following:

- the standards for QTS;
- the requirements of the induction year;
- the forthcoming OFSTED inspection.

Where do you go from here? Consider the following options:

- another observation for Jeremy in the near future;
- involving the head of the geography department;
- involving a member of the senior leadership team;
- contacting the local education authority about your concerns.

You decide to arrange another observation with Jeremy. You tell him in writing that you will observe a Year 11 class in two weeks' time. This is the memo you send.

Jeremy

Further to my recent observation of your Year 8 class and the subsequent feedback, I feel that it would be beneficial to observe you again in two weeks' time with your Year 11 class. In this observation I will be focusing on the following with respect to the standards required for QTS:

- 1.7 An ability to improve your own teaching by evaluating it with particular reference to a positive response from the feedback of others.
- 3.1.2 Use of teaching and learning objectives in the planning of lessons.
- 3.1.3 Selection and preparation of resources that take into account pupils' interests and their language backgrounds.
- 3.2.1 Appropriate use of monitoring and assessment strategies to evaluate pupils' progress.

I hope that you feel that your induction is going well and that you are settling into the school.

May I also take this opportunity of reminding you that the LEA has organised a session on behaviour management for all NQTs next Thursday at 4 p.m. and a place has been reserved for you on this course.

If you feel that you need any further help please do not hesitate to contact me.

Yours

A professional mentor
cc Head of geography

Feedback form

Feedback to Jeremy: September/October. Year 8 geography class/Year 11 geography top set

Year 8	Year 11
Professional values and practice:	Professional values and practice:
Knowledge and understanding:	Knowledge and understanding:
Teaching:	Teaching:

Jeremy receives the memo

The memo is placed in Jeremy's pigeon-hole. At lunchtime you enter the staff room to witness Jeremy in full flow with an audience that includes the other NQTs. He sees you enter and approaches you, angrily waving the memo. You remain calm and ask Jeremy to accompany you to a private office where you both sit down. The walk to the office has the desired effect and Jeremy is calmer. You ask him why there is a problem with your intention to observe him again. To your surprise it is not the observation that concerns Jeremy but the fact that he has had a place reserved for him on a behaviour management course. He explains at length that having served in the army as a commissioned officer he has no need to participate in such a course. In fact, it would be more appropriate if he himself were leading the course.

Task three

Consider how you could convince Jeremy of the need to participate in the course. How would you differentiate between his experiences of behaviour management in the army and the requirements of the school? In addition, you will need to address Jeremy's outburst in the staff room.

Week four: Jeremy's second observation

After the incident in the staff room and your subsequent meeting with Jeremy there appears to be an improvement. He was apologetic about his public display of dissatisfaction in the staff room and assured you that, if he had any further concerns, he would see you directly and not broadcast his views to other members of staff. He attended the course on behaviour management and his feedback to you afterwards was very positive: he identified a number of strategies that had been suggested and that he intended to use in his own practice.

Jeremy is also becoming involved in the school's Duke of Edinburgh Award scheme and has indicated his desire to participate in a forthcoming weekend expedition. You are delighted when you hear this as Jeremy's previous experiences mean that he has much to offer in this area.

You arrive at the Year 11 lesson for the second observation. Jeremy is already in the class and there is a PowerPoint presentation at the ready. The first slide clearly shows the lesson objectives.

The class enter the room in an orderly manner and there is an obvious workmanlike and professional atmosphere in the class. With this older age group Jeremy is able to relate to the class though it appears that in questioning he favours the boys and rarely asks girls to contribute.

The lesson progresses well with a variety of tasks. Transitions are smooth and there is a useful plenary that relates appropriately to the lesson objectives. Jeremy has used ICT effectively to enhance learning and pupils have had to interpret statistical data.

You leave the lesson delighted and you feel that this high-ability GCSE class has benefited from the learning and teaching evident in Jeremy's lesson.

Prepare written feedback for Jeremy using the Feedback form (page 43). You should refer to the standards for QTS and decide which Jeremy is meeting and how well. It will be useful for you to have the copy of your previous observation notes for the Year 8 class to hand.

The meeting with Jeremy goes well. You say you were delighted with the lesson and also his contribution to the corporate life of the school through the Duke of Edinburgh Award scheme. Half term arrives and you feel more satisfied with your relationship with Jeremy. However, you are conscious of the OFSTED inspection that will take place three weeks after the half term holiday.

An inspector calls

It is a tense time at Countryside Comprehensive School. It is the week of the OFSTED inspection. On Monday morning you observe Jeremy in the staff room, with an audience as usual, announcing his lack of concern about the inspection week. As the new professional mentor you do not share his confidence: your procedures and strategies for induction are going to be under close scrutiny. You feel that you have done a good job with the other NQTs, who are more appreciative of the efforts that you have made on their behalf. You overhear Jeremy saying that he is going to 'carry on as normal' and that he has little time for 'those not in the front line.'

It is not long before your worst fears materialise. On Monday afternoon you see an inspector entering Jeremy's classroom. With disquiet you consult the timetable and find that Jeremy is teaching his low-ability Year 9 class.

At the end of school you wait to ask Jeremy how the inspector's observation has gone. It is over an hour before he and the inspector emerge from the lesson.

Jeremy storms straight past you and heads for the car park: he leaves the school, his tyres screeching. Meanwhile, an ashen-faced inspector makes for the headteacher's office.

The following morning you receive the following memo in your internal mail.

Dear Professional Mentor

The geography inspector would like to meet you in your role as professional mentor re: your perceptions of Jeremy's progress as an NQT. I will also be present at the meeting in my office at 1 p.m.

Yours

A headteacher

At the meeting the headteacher explains that there were 'certain concerns' about Jeremy's lesson with the low-ability Year 9 class. The inspector would like your perceptions of Jeremy's progress and evidence of written reports within 24 hours.

Prepare a written statement of your perceptions of Jeremy as an NQT. You should aim to write 250–300 words based on your observations so far. You may like to consider the following:

- *your first impressions of Jeremy;*
- *the observation of the Year 8 class;*
- *the observation of the Year 11 class;*
- *Jeremy's relationships with other staff in the common room;*
- *Jeremy's career aspirations.*

You meet the headteacher and the inspector the following day as arranged. You give them your report. Within the parameters of confidentiality the headteacher and the inspector explain their concerns, which may be summarised as follows:

'An arrogant individual who lacked empathy and understanding of this group. No attempt was made to include all pupils. Tasks were inappropriate and beyond the level of all pupils in the class. A total lack of evidence of any cross-curricular themes. Overall a lesson that lacked any structure with no evidence either to the pupils or the observer of objectives or progression.'

End piece

The final meeting with Jeremy went well and he agreed that he was intolerant of pupils of low ability. Though concerns were expressed in his first induction report at the end of the autumn term he did in fact go on to achieve QTS at the end of his first year. This was due to a detailed training plan designed by the professional mentor and to Jeremy's own determination after the shock of the inspector's observations. Jeremy's Year 11 class achieved 100 per cent success at GCSE A*–C, with ten pupils achieving A*.

7   The language of life

Intended learning outcomes

This is a classic case where a mentor is faced with a considerable challenge when a young teacher behaves inappropriately outside the classroom. The mentor will develop an awareness of conflict management strategies and begin to define the range and scope of a subject mentor's responsibilities.

Setting the scene

This case study explores the challenge of managing a talented young teacher who, in his first term of full-time employment as a teacher of English at Hightown High School, uses verbal and physical aggression towards a Year 11 pupil. The school has a very good reputation in the area. In the past five years, under a new headteacher, it has acquired specialist school status and raised pupil attainment remarkably. It is over-subscribed, with a very active parent teacher association.

There is no doubt that the teacher's actions are a cause for concern and possibly disciplinary proceedings. However, the pupil is a notoriously disaffected and disruptive character with a history including fixed-term exclusions for foul and abusive language to members of staff. The teacher has made a very encouraging start to his career and is well regarded by both pupils and staff alike.

Hightown has a well-established induction programme in that NQTs are allocated to a subject mentor who is, in turn, managed by a professional mentor (a member of the senior Leadership Team). In this case study, the headteacher, in consultation with the professional mentor, has agreed that the most judicious and sensitive approach would be to ask the subject mentor to initiate discussions with the teacher about his alleged misconduct.

All subject mentors at Hightown have received training before taking on this role, including lesson observation skills, counselling, and the LEA programme on the transition from ITT to induction with a full awareness of the national standards for confirmation of QTS at the end of the first year of teaching.

The NQT induction programme at Hightown has been recognised, within the LEA, as a model of good practice. Indeed, in the school's last OFSTED inspection, the programme was singled out for particular praise as it involved a large number of school staff (both teaching and non-teaching) and also made a significant contribution to the school's award of Investors in People. All NQTs, as part of the programme, receive an individual seminar with their subject mentor on a weekly basis: this provides an opportunity to discuss progress towards the standards and to raise any other professional issues of concern to either party.

Given this highly professional environment, it is essential to consider the parameters of the subject mentor's role. Hightown has developed a job specification for subject mentors. The preamble to the job description is:

Hightown expects subject mentors to work in a close professional relationship with an NQT to ensure that he/she receives the support and guidance required to achieve the induction standards at the end of the first year of teaching. The school recognises that mentoring is a complex and demanding role. Subject mentors are given considerable autonomy in the management of their NQTs. Although final assessment remains the responsibility of the headteacher, in reality subject mentors will provide the necessary evidence upon which this decision will be made and will also have to operate as a critical friend, coach, adviser, counsellor and tutor. The professional mentor's key responsibility is not only to ensure uniformity and consistency of provision for all NQTs, but to recognise the different contexts within the school and to be sensitive to the nature of these professional relationships.

The incident

Peter Baggley has been in Hightown High School for six weeks. He has made an excellent start to his teaching career. His work in English at both Key Stage 3 and Key Stage 4 has shown close attention to detail. His preparation, planning and resource generation are excellent. His marking is thorough. His performance in the classroom is very assured and confident. He expects (and largely achieves) pupil behaviour of the highest order. This is probably a by-product of Peter's maturity and (to some extent) his sheer physical presence. He is a former semi-professional rugby league player. He has already started a junior rugby league team in the school and the boys are rather in awe of him. His mentor enjoys working with Peter although she realises that he has some very fixed views about the role of a teacher.

On Friday of last week the headteacher received a letter from the father of a Year 11 boy alleging Peter had used foul and abusive language to his son. Peter allegedly called the boy a 'stupid little p***k'. The father expects the school to take some disciplinary action. The headteacher asks the subject mentor to investigate and submit a report within two days.

The evidence is incontrovertible. Peter was on dinner queue duty and the boy (SW) jumped the queue in an effort to get an early lunch. Peter spotted him and moved him to the back of the queue. The boy tried the same trick again and Peter became irritated, grabbed the boy by his arm and took him to the back of the queue for the second time. The boy did not like his treatment and resisted, calling Peter a 'f***ing bully'. It was at this point that Peter switched his grip to the boy's collar, called him a 'stupid little p***k,' stood him against a wall and told him he would be the last pupil to enter the dining hall. This information was obtained from reliable pupil witnesses and a trusted welfare assistant who were interviewed by the professional mentor.

> **Task one**
>
> *Explore the head teacher's expectation that the subject mentor should deal with the parental complaint in the first instance.*
>
> - *What impact could this have on the relationship between Peter and his mentor?*
> - *Is this an appropriate task to delegate? Is it a recognition of mentoring skills or is it an unfair burden?*

Monday afternoon

Despite several reservations, the subject mentor accepts the headteacher's request and sends the following letter to Peter Baggley.

Dear Peter,

I would like to meet you tomorrow (Tuesday) at 10.30 a.m. in the Professional Development Centre to discuss a letter of complaint received from SW's father (I have attached a copy for you). The purpose of the meeting is to give you an opportunity to present your side of the story. The matter is confidential. Please do not speak to SW. This meeting is not part of the school's disciplinary procedure. I have been asked by the headteacher to investigate these allegations and submit a full and detailed report. He feels it is appropriate that I do this as your subject mentor.

Yours sincerely

A Mentor

Dear Headteacher,

My son was verbally abused and manhandled by a member of your staff yesterday while he was in the dinner queue. His name is Mr Baggley and lots of people witnessed his disgraceful behaviour. I expect something to be done and quickly. Teachers are not allowed to use force with pupils and my son was very upset and when he finally got into the dining hall there was no food left so he had to make do with a sandwich. My son likes school and he has never been in serious trouble and if I do not get this thing sorted out, there will be trouble.

Yours sincerely

Mr SW

Peter Baggley received the letters in his pigeon-hole at 4.30 p.m. on Monday.

> **Task two**
>
> *Should the mentor have communicated differently?*

Tuesday morning

Peter speaks to you in the staff room and informs you that he intends to see SW's father on a man-to-man basis to 'sort this nonsense out'. He also tells you that SW is taunting him and he will not stand for it. This is an unexpected development.

Later on Tuesday morning Peter's union representative advises you that the matter has been referred to his regional office as Peter feels he is being unfairly treated and that the correct procedures have not been followed by the school. Peter has agreed to attend the meeting at 10.30 a.m. accompanied by his union representative who has told you (off the record) that he is eager to see the matter resolved before it becomes unnecessarily painful and blown out of all proportion.

Task three

Should the subject mentor consider the following possibilities?

- *seeking the support of other staff;*
- *redefining the rules of confidentiality;*
- *preventing escalation (Peter's expressed intention to confront SW's father).*

The headteacher's damage limitation

The subject mentor decides to delay the meeting until she has spoken to the headteacher. She learns that the headteacher has spoken to SW's father, confirmed that the school is investigating the matter thoroughly and stated that the school has clear rules on the conduct of its staff and that abusive language and physical assault are not acceptable. He has assured the parent that the appropriate disciplinary action will be taken if the teacher concerned is indeed guilty of the allegations made. He has made it clear that this would probably involve a formal warning.

The headteacher has also spoken to the father about his son's inappropriate behaviour and rudeness which provoked the situation. He has emphasised Mr Baggley's excellent work in the school and reminded the father that Mr Baggley is nevertheless a very inexperienced teacher in his first six weeks of teaching. He emphasises that Mr Baggley has an excellent career in front of him.

The father accepts that the school will deal with the matter but expects the school to keep him informed of the outcomes. The headteacher talks to the subject mentor, explaining the conversation with SW's father. He asks her to speak to Peter Baggley to gain his full understanding of the implications of his actions and to ensure further training for him in the management of challenging behaviour.

The headteacher is well aware that incidents like this stem from normal human behaviour. He wants to be assured of no further repetition and that Peter really appreciates the expectations placed on him by the school, parents and the law.

In the light of this information the subject mentor has to reschedule her meeting with Peter. Peter agrees to meet later in the week but his union representative will still join him in the discussion and has confirmed that Peter will make no direct contact with SW's father.

Task four

Now consider the developing situation from Peter's perspective. The questions below are at the forefront of his thinking.

What outcomes should the subject mentor be working towards? You should begin to anticipate likely concerns and uncertainties. The questions that Peter Baggley is likely to ask himself will assist you in your thinking. Prepare for the meeting.

- *Am I going to be formally disciplined?*
- *Why is this matter not being dealt with personally by the head teacher?*
- *Has the school followed the correct procedure for dealing with complaints from parents?*
- *What action has been taken with pupil SW? He seems to have got off very lightly.*
- *Will this meeting be minuted and a record kept? If so, who will have access to it?*
- *What happens at the end of this meeting?*
- *Will this incident go on my personal file?*
- *Will I get to see the information passed on to SW's father?*

End piece

Peter Baggley was formally disciplined by the headteacher. He was given a verbal warning about his conduct in the SW incident and his future conduct. He accepted this with good grace.

He was directed towards in-house training, working with staff experienced in dealing with challenging behaviour.

His relationship with his mentor was not easily restored to its former level as both the mentor and Peter felt that the experience had undermined the fundamental purposes behind mentoring. Nevertheless they continued to work together professionally and Peter successfully completed his NQT year.

Peter's junior rugby league team was very successful and earned a reputation of playing a hard but fair game.

Peter gained promotion to a neighbouring school after only four terms at Hightown. He is rumoured to be making quite an impression as assistant head of year.

8 Carrie Anne: Oh yes I will, oh no I won't

Intended learning outcomes

The main purpose of this case study is to invite discussion about the principles that a mentor should uphold in relationships with other key stakeholders when a trainee, motivated by understandable self-interest and naivety, acts unprofessionally.

Setting the scene

As professional mentor you are pleased to hear from one of your colleagues in another school that you will be joined by Carrie Anne for her second placement. Carrie Anne has completed her first placement at your colleague's school and describes her as one of the best trainees that she has ever mentored 'who will be an asset to the teaching profession.' Her only regret is that her own school does not have a current vacancy as Carrie Anne would be a very strong candidate.

Carrie Anne is a mature student who left school at 16 with a limited number of GCEs and CSEs. Having married and had a family she has committed herself to joining the teaching profession. This has not been easy for her. After supplementing her qualifications at GCSE level and completing three A levels at evening classes, she gained a place at a prestigious local university and gained a first class honours degree in information and communication studies. She is currently completing her PGCE at your partnership HEI.

Your school is an 11–16 mixed comprehensive. It is situated in an urban area of deprivation. There are 750 pupils with an intake of 150 pupils per year group. An indication of social deprivation is reflected in the following statistics:

- 50 per cent of pupils are entitled to free school dinners;
- 20 per cent of pupils are from one parent families;
- unemployment in the area is well above the national average.

Despite these figures the school is achieving well. Thirty two per cent of pupils achieved 5 A*–C GCSEs in the previous year, an increase of 15 per cent over the last three years. For the first time in its history the school is over-subscribed and its reputation is rising. This is due partly to the extremely effective and professional leadership team, of which you are a member as professional mentor. The school is held in high esteem by the partnership HEI for its involvement in initial teacher training. Indeed, within your organisation ITT is seen as a significant element in school improvement and is fully integrated into the school improvement plan. The ICT department which Carrie Anne will be joining, is particularly effective in the training of teachers, with an experienced subject mentor who also serves on the subject panel of the ICT department at the partnership HEI.

The week before Carrie Anne arrives at your school you receive her reports from her first placement school and from the college. Your colleague was certainly not exaggerating. Carrie Anne is making excellent progress, is working to all the standards for qualified teacher status and is performing at a level well above what could be reasonably expected at this point in her course. You look forward to meeting her.

When Carrie Anne arrives at the school you are not disappointed. She is immaculately dressed, has an imposing presence and the air of a true professional. In your induction sessions she appears somewhat modest but clearly very willing to learn, asking appropriate questions and contributing intelligently to discussion sessions as trainees reflect upon their experiences of their first placement.

The views from your fellow professional mentor and the college reports bode well for the future. However, as this case study develops you will be met with a number of challenges that will test your mentoring skills in deciding whether Carrie Anne is meeting the following standards for QTS:

1.3 They demonstrate and promote positive values, attitudes and behaviour that they expect from pupils.

1.5 They can contribute to and share responsibility in the corporate life of the school.

1.7 They are able to improve their own teaching, by evaluating it, learning from the effective practice of others and from evidence. They are motivated and able to take increasing responsibility for their own professional development.

The end of week one of the placement

You have your weekly meeting with the ICT subject mentor. She expresses her delight at the way that Carrie Anne is settling into the school and the department. After a week's observation the subject mentor is so confident that Carrie Anne has a full understanding of the classes that she is teaching that she anticipates Carrie Anne will be able to teach her classes independently after a further week's collaborative teaching.

Task one

In collaboration with the subject mentor your task is to devise a programme of development for this talented trainee. You should take into account the following:

- *her accelerated progress so far;*
- *methods to develop further her obvious potential;*
- *ways in which she can contribute and share responsibility for the corporate life of the school within the parameters of standard 1.5: 'They can contribute to and share responsibility in the corporate life of the school.'*

Week three of the placement

For the trainees at your school the time has arrived to apply for their first teaching posts. They are naturally anxious about this process. Despite the fact that they have had some limited advice from their college about applications, they request a professional studies session with you to give the school's point of view.

Task two

Devise a session for the trainees that will provide advice on how to go about applying for their first teaching post. Consider the following:

- *where to look for posts;*
- *the letter of application;*
- *the interview process;*
- *the protocols involved in the application for teaching posts;*
- *who else you may involve in the session.*

The session goes particularly well and the trainees seem pleased with your input. However, you are a little concerned that Carrie Anne has failed to attend the session. This is most out of character as you had seen her in school that morning and spoken briefly to her about the afternoon's session. On reflection you realise that she had been somewhat non-committal during the conversation.

Task three

You decide that you need to speak to Carrie Anne about her non-attendance at your mentoring session. As there could be a perfectly reasonable explanation for her absence you decide to wait 24 hours for Carrie Anne to approach you. As no approach is made you ask to see her in your office after school, explaining the reason for the meeting.

Carrie Anne fails to turn up for the meeting and as you are leaving school you find the following note in your pigeon-hole:

Dear Professional Mentor

I do not intend to meet you after school today as I do not see the need for such a meeting. This is much in the same way that I did not need to attend your mentoring session on job applications.

I have a great deal of experience in the commercial world and I am fully aware of how to apply for a post. Furthermore, I feel that my ability, which you have so often praised, will ensure that I have no problem in securing a position.

I felt that my time was put to better use in preparing lessons.

Yours truly,

Carrie Anne

Considering Carrie Anne's past record of compliance and excellent potential this note takes you by surprise, particularly her assertions that she did not need any help in applying for posts and that her time was better spent in lesson preparation. For the first time you see another side to Carrie Anne's character.

Decide how you would deal with this unexpected response and the need to have a meeting with Carrie Anne. You may wish to consider the following:

- *Carrie Anne's excellent record so far;*
- *the lack of professional etiquette in failing to turn up for a meeting;*

- *the arrogance of her actions;*
- *the lack of courtesy in not attending without explanation both before the session and after;*
- *whether you should meet her alone.*

Once you have decided to meet Carrie Anne you should consider what her concerns are likely to be before the rearranged meeting. For example:

- *Am I going to be asked to leave the school/course?*
- *How will my future be affected?*
- *What is going to happen to me at the end of this meeting?*
- *I do not believe that I have been unreasonable.*

In fact, the meeting goes well as a result of your strategies and you are pleased with the outcome. Your emphasis on Carrie Anne's successes and her potential convince her of the error of her actions. She apologises and assures you there will be no repetition of this behaviour. You point out that her actions could have resulted in disciplinary procedures if she had been a qualified teacher. Carrie Anne is left in no doubt that her actions were wrong.

Four weeks later

You decided not to inform the college of Carrie Anne's actions in missing your mentoring session and the subsequent meeting. You feel that your decision is justified as she continues to make excellent progress and has become a valuable member of the ICT department. Furthermore, she is contributing to the after-school computer club. She has assisted in devising a new scheme of work for Key Stage 3 pupils and has worked closely with an experienced teacher. His contact with Carrie Anne has re-energised his approach to teaching, resulting in his questioning his own practice and reflecting upon his rather staid lessons. The subject mentor and the head of department are delighted with Carrie Anne's progress and her overall contribution to teaching and learning within the department.

Carrie Anne informs you that she is interested in a post for a newly qualified teacher that she has seen advertised. She asks you to act as a referee for her application and particularly asks whether or not you would feel it necessary to mention the previous unfortunate incident. You are delighted for Carrie Anne but feel that there are certain caveats you should mention about the school to which she intends to apply. It is a 30-mile journey from her home, it has been in special measures and there are regular reports in the local newspaper about a prevalent drug culture in the school. Despite this, Carrie Anne is adamant that she would like to make an application. You wish her well. She is successful at the interview and secures the post.

Two weeks later

You are a little concerned that Carrie Anne has had six days' absence from school since her interview (she has phoned in sick). You become even more concerned when a member of staff returns from a school visit to a local theme park and reports that he saw Carrie Anne there with her own family enjoying the white-knuckle rides. Carrie Anne returns to school two days later.

Consider the following questions:

- *What should your actions be in response to this latest incident?*
- *How do you approach Carrie Anne, bearing in mind that you have already experienced an unsavoury side to her character?*
- *Is the positive nature of your reference for Carrie Anne jeopardising your own professional integrity in any way?*
- *Is it necessary to inform the college of this latest incident?*

You meet Carrie Anne who admits that she was at the theme park. She explains that it was her daughter's birthday and although she was still feeling ill she did not want to let her daughter down. As professional mentor you are unconvinced by this explanation. Consider the actions that you will take.

A further two weeks later

Your meeting with Carrie Anne confirms your concerns about her understanding of the nature of professionalism. You contact the college and informally report your concerns, again emphasising the potential that Carrie Anne has shown in her pursuit of a teaching career so far. The college tutor acknowledges your concerns but gives you the impression that you are over-reacting to the situation. Your concerns are exacerbated when the ICT subject mentor informs you that Carrie Anne has failed to sign the contract for the post that she accepted verbally some weeks ago. Furthermore, the subject mentor confides in you that Carrie Anne has heard on the grapevine about another post that will be available for an ICT teacher in a prestigious local girls' private school. This would enable Carrie Anne to secure an assisted place for her daughter at the school and avoid travelling to the school where she has already verbally accepted a post. Eventually Carrie Anne approaches you and explains the situation.

Carrie Anne asks if you will be prepared to act as referee for her application to the second post.

Decide what your response to this request will be and give reasons for your decision.

You decide that providing a reference will put your own professional reputation at risk. Therefore you decline to provide a reference, explaining your reasons and emphasising your growing concerns about Carrie Anne's professionalism in the light of other developments since her appointment to the post. Carrie Anne leaves your office clearly annoyed by your response.

Later that day you receive a telephone call from Carrie Anne's tutor saying that she is willing to support Carrie Anne's application, without reference to the appointment that Carrie Anne has already accepted. You explain that you cannot put your own professional reputation at risk and that you are disappointed with the attitude of the college. The tutor asks if you are prepared to write to the second school simply saying that Carrie Anne has proved to be an excellent classroom practitioner.

Decide on your response to this request from the college tutor.

One week later

You write the following reference for Carrie Anne:

> Dear Headteacher
>
> Carrie Anne is in the process of completing her second block practice at my school. She has many attributes in terms of her ability but I have doubts about her professionalism. For example, I am aware that she has already accepted a post for September at a local comprehensive school.
>
> Yours faithfully
>
> A professional mentor

Despite this communication with the school, Carrie Anne is called for interview. She returns to your school the following day and informs the subject mentor that she has been successful at the interview and accepted the post. The subject mentor relays this information to you. You ask to see Carrie Anne straight away.

During the meeting Carrie Anne is adamant that she will accept the second post for personal reasons. You emphasise that she must contact the first school and explain immediately that she will be not be taking the post: after all, this is six weeks after her initial interview and verbal acceptance of the post. Carrie Anne promises to do this.

Despite her promises you feel that as professional mentor, and to protect your own reputation, you should speak to the headteacher of the first school explaining your disappointment with Carrie Anne's attitude. The headteacher is delighted to receive your support and you discover that Carrie Anne has not been truthful but has said that her husband has been relocated to another area of the country and that she will be unable to take the job.

Task six

Although there are only two weeks left in the practice, you are becoming increasingly frustrated with Carrie Anne's actions. You call her back into your office and demand an explanation in the presence of the subject mentor. What will be the result of the meeting?

End piece

Carrie Anne was asked to leave the school immediately. The college was contacted and told of the decision. They were sympathetic towards Carrie Anne and concerned that she should be able to complete her course. Carrie Anne made arrangements to complete her final two weeks at the school where she had been a pupil. Both the partnership school and the school where Carrie Anne had accepted the post expressed their concerns to the college who, at directorate level, accepted the criticisms of the behaviour of one of their trainees. Nevertheless, Carrie Anne was able to pursue a career in teaching at a prestigious girls' private school and no doubt enjoy the advantages of reduced fees for her daughter.

9   Not-so-sweet Caroline

Intended learning outcomes

Caroline's story enables participants to recognise that successful mentoring needs a profile of personal skills and qualities to complement professional expertise in pedagogy and practice.

Setting the scene

Partnerships between HEIs and schools are the organisational basis for practice in teacher education. These partnerships will only be successful if school personnel are able to engage in developmental mentoring that is sympathetic to the needs of the trainee and supportive in terms of providing realistic targets for progression and the meeting of the standards required for QTS.

Roles and tasks

Within this case study the central theme will consider the role of the mentor in terms of the establishment of a working relationship with the trainee. Of particular relevance will be the mentor's ability to relate to the following roles and tasks recognised as being of importance to the establishment of working practice within the partnerships:

Coach/trainer: lead reviews, evaluate trainee performance and competence, write reports.

Assessor: observe trainee teaching.

Lakeside Comprehensive School has recently entered an ITT partnership with its local HEI. The school could be described as a late starter in ITT but nevertheless the senior leadership team are determined to make the partnership work and reap the benefits for professional development and school improvement associated with such a partnership. Caroline, an assistant headteacher at Lakeside, has taken on the role of professional mentor and received two days' training at the partnership HEI. Caroline had no previous experience of mentoring and the course that the HEI provided was largely for dealing with administrative and procedural matters associated with the role of professional mentor. There was little if any preparation for mastering the skills associated with challenging moments in mentoring. Caroline is enthusiastic about the prospect of taking on the mentoring role with trainees.

 Caroline is a high flyer. She has been teaching for ten years, all of them at Lakeside where she began her teaching career as a newly qualified teacher in mathematics. She progressed to head of mathematics after only four years and, despite ruffling a few feathers, reorganised the department to become one of the most successful in the school. Her work ethos and competence cannot be doubted, although there are question marks about her relationships with other teaching staff and her lack of ability to empathise with others. Many staff had doubts about Caroline's appointment to the post of professional mentor. However, Caroline is ambitious and saw it as an important step in her career progression. She was appointed following an internal interview. Her attitudes to others will be seriously tested as this case study unfolds.

Task one

Caroline returns to Lakeside School after her mentor training and is asked by the head-teacher to make a presentation to the senior leadership team about the advantages and benefits that accrue from partnership. Consider how Caroline would address the relevant points and how they may be implemented from a practical point of view at Lakeside School.

Advantages of ITT partnerships	Disadvantages of ITT partnerships

---

All appears well for the trainees

It is the first day for the trainees at Lakeside School. Caroline has arranged an intensive induction programme that will involve the trainees getting a feel for the school. At the end of the day the trainees are impressed by both the school and the arrangements that have been made by Caroline. Caroline's organisational abilities and confidence are evident despite her being new to the position of professional mentor. In the first few weeks the trainees settle well, following a detailed programme of observation, collaborative planning and general professional studies. At these sessions they report that they feel valued in the school and appreciate the time and effort that Caroline and her team of subject mentors are giving to their development.

Week five of the practice

Caroline is delighted with the way that the first five weeks have gone from the point of view of her new role and the way that the trainees have settled within the school. It is now time for the trainees to teach alone in lessons under the supervision of a mentor. Caroline organises a programme of lesson observations that she will undertake and that will include detailed feedback following the lessons. Observation and feedback are complex skills for which training and practice are required. It must be remembered that the process is useful for the trainees in their development and that it is for their benefit. Earley and Bubb (2004) in their book *Leading and Managing Continuing Professional Development* outline the following important considerations in the context of the observation:

- the stage of the trainee (is this an early or final teaching practice?);
- how they are feeling;
- their previous experience of being observed (if any);
- the state of the mentor's relationship with the trainee;
- what part of the school year, week and day it happens in;
- the disposition of the class.

Task two

Caroline is going to observe Joanna, a trainee German teacher, take a difficult Year 9 class. She needs to prepare herself and Joanna for the observation. As Caroline, consider how you would go about this preparation and design your plan using the following headings:

- *before the observation;*
- *during the observation;*
- *how your observation will be recorded;*
- *after the observation – how it will be discussed.*

Consider in particular:

- *What will your focus in the lesson be?*
- *How detailed and appropriate is the lesson plan?*
- *How will you gather evidence?*
- *What steps will you take to be unobtrusive?*
- *What questions will you raise in the post-lesson feedback?*

Feedback time: Caroline shows her true colours

Remember that Caroline is a perfectionist. Although Joanna feels that the lesson went well Caroline does not share these views. She attacks Joanna's lesson by pointing out the following errors:

> 'There was an obvious nervousness in your approach to the lesson and the pupils were fully aware of this. The start of the lesson was delayed by the late arrival of five boys from PE. Explanations lacked clarity, as did a clear outline of the lesson objectives and outcomes. Questioning was ad hoc and did not involve the majority of the class. Your voice was mono-tonal and the pupils failed to respond to your input: two pupils at the back of the class constantly sent messages on their mobile phones. Group work was badly organised and failed to realise your desired learning outcomes. Time management was poor and you failed to include a meaningful plenary. There are many areas of development that will need to be addressed if you are to meet the standards of QTS as outlined in your ITT handbook.'

Caroline rushes off at the end of the lesson and leaves this note with the subject mentor, in a sealed envelope, asking him to pass it on to Joanna with the message that she would like to see Joanna the following day at lunchtime.

> ### Task three
>
> *Joanna opens the envelope and immediately bursts into tears in the presence of the sub-ject mentor. She shows Caroline's feedback notes to the subject mentor. The subject mentor is incensed by the feedback. Consider the feedback and the method of passing it to Joanna.*
>
> - *How should the professional mentor have approached the content of the written feed-back and arrangements for verbal feedback?*
> - *What are the essential requirements necessary for lesson observations to be develop-mental?*
>
> *Though the content of the written feedback may be accurate, it cannot be described as helpful in developing Joanna. Rewrite this feedback in different language that would motivate Joanna rather than destroy her confidence.*
>
> *Consider also the questions that you would raise for Joanna at the verbal feedback in order to enable her to reflect upon this lesson. You may find it useful to refer to the con-siderations for lesson observations outlined earlier in the chapter.*

The professional mentor exerts authority over the subject mentor

The subject mentor has been delighted with Joanna's progress and her contribution to the school so far. She has listened to and acted upon advice from the modern foreign languages department after observations and collaborative planning and shown a keen desire to be involved in other aspects of school life. She has attended open evenings and parents' evenings and as a joint graduate in German and Arabic started a lunchtime Arabic club. The subject mentor is annoyed at the effect that Caroline's observation has had upon Joanna.

He immediately seeks out Caroline and challenges her on her approach to Joanna and her means of communication. Caroline is adamant that she is merely following guidelines from the partnership college and maintaining the standards for QTS. Caroline is unrepentant about her methods of feedback and communication explaining that she is a very busy person and her role goes far beyond the parameters of simply being a professional mentor within Lakeside School. She concludes that as she has so many concerns about Joanna she will be formally observing her again in two weeks' time and will expect a 'big improvement.'

Two weeks later

The subject mentor has worked with Joanna over the last two weeks to restore her confi-dence, and observations by him and other members of the department have been very positive. Joanna has worked well to achieve the necessary standards. The subject mentor has advised Joanna on the lesson that is to be observed by Caroline and a detailed lesson plan is in place. The day for the observation arrives and Caroline is in the classroom as the Year 7 mixed-ability group arrives for their German lesson. Joanna has the learning objectives clearly visible on the board. She is naturally nervous about this observation but her subject mentor has assured her that she has the capabilities to be a good teacher and that all will go well. The pupils enjoy the lesson on the use of numbers in German and all seems well.

However, Caroline does not view the lesson in the same way and, although she gives verbal feedback immediately after the lesson, it is far from supportive and her written notes are less than complimentary.

Task four

Study the contents of Caroline's written feedback relating to the standards for qualified teacher status.

Lesson Observation of Year 7 German class: achievement of standards for QTS

Professional values and practice

Standard 1.2 Builds relationship with pupils that are positive
Showed little interest in the pupils within the class.
Standard 1.6 Develops highly effective working relationships with support staff
Limited use of the SSA.
Standard 1.7 Production of lesson evaluations
No evidence of progression from previous lesson with this class.

Knowledge and understanding

Standard 2.1 Demonstrates a strong and secure knowledge of their subject
Pupils understood numbers 1–20 in German.
Standard 2.4 Demonstrates a good knowledge of the different levels of development and ability of pupils
There was little evidence of differentiation within this lesson.
Standard 2.7 Maintains effective discipline throughout the lesson
Two pupils were off task.

Teaching

Standard 3.1.3 Selects interesting and appropriate resources to deliver the lessons
Use of football scores not appropriate to teach numbers.
Standard 3.2.2 Provides effective feedback to pupils as a regular feature of the lesson
Over-use of praise.
Standard 3.3.1 Makes full and effective use of awards and sanctions
Over-use of merits.

Areas for development
See above.

Joanna is naturally devastated by this written feedback and the verbal feedback is merely a repetition of the written notes. Joanna has no opportunity to respond or reflect and the entire process takes less than five minutes.
  How would you improve this feedback to Joanna? Consider particularly the needs of trainees if feedback is to be developmental.

Has Joanna reached the end of the line?

At the end of the day Joanna returns to college to seek out her tutor. She shows him the lesson observation notes and explains that although the school in general and the department in particular are supportive she finds the professional mentor totally negative. She feels that she can no longer continue either at the school or on the PGCE course despite her continued desire to join the teaching profession. Joanna has always been considered a model student by the college and the tutor is sympathetic. He decides upon the following course of action.

He will contact the school and arrange to attend an observation in the following week. The class to be observed will be a parallel Year 7 group and Joanna will teach the same lesson again. The tutor will request that Caroline participates in joint observation and joint feedback.

He assures Joanna that the lesson plan is appropriate and that she can rely upon the support of the college. The tutor contacts the school and arrangements are made for the subsequent observation.

Task five

Do you consider this the best way forward in order to restore Joanna's confidence? You may like to consider the issues of professionalism, partnership and transparency that are involved in this decision. What alternatives would you consider at this stage?

One week later

Despite your answers to Task five, the tutor goes ahead with his decision. It is time for the joint observation.

As instructed by the tutor, Joanna teaches the lesson in much the same way as the previous week. Throughout the lesson Caroline's face and body language indicate her realisation that there has been collaboration between Joanna and her tutor. She is naturally angry and this becomes evident at the feedback session. The tutor briefly meets Caroline alone before this session and presents her with the following written feedback that he intends to focus upon with Joanna.

Summary of classroom obervation

Joanna, this was an excellent lesson in which the pupils were fully engaged. I feel that I now have a full knowledge of not only numbers in German but also their application. The following points are particularly of note in your development at this stage of your training:

- a workmanlike atmosphere in that all pupils remained on task;
- the ability of the pupils to relate to the subject matter through everyday experiences (football results on this occasion);
- an ability to empathise with the pupils: smiling, encouraging, supporting, facial expressions, etc;
- involvement of all pupils in your question and answer sessions;
- excellent transition between activities reflecting a good understanding of the need for variety in lessons;
- good references to numeracy;
- time management was generally good (however, see below);
- resources were well planned and appropriate.

Areas for development

- Though you made the learning objectives clear at the beginning of the lesson, you must return to these as the lesson progresses.
- You must ensure that there is sufficient time for a meaningful plenary – pupils must leave the room knowing what they have learned.
- Make even more use of the support teacher.

Objectives

Ensure that you act upon the observations noted above and understand how they are transferable to other lessons/classes that you teach.

Task six

Compare this written feedback with Caroline's earlier observations. You may like to consider the following questions.

- How does it encourage Joanna to reflect?
- What questions would you as college tutor raise in order for Joanna to improve her practice?
- How might Joanna feel after this feedback compared with her previous experiences?

End piece

Caroline is appalled by the approach that the tutor has taken. She realises that her own way of working has been questioned and after refusing to attend the feedback session for Joanna she immediately goes to see the headteacher. He listens to her concerns and realises that the incident has made one of his senior staff extremely angry. He contacts the college and after heated negotiations it is decided that the partnership cannot continue during this academic year. Joanna completes her first practice at another school and continues to complete her PGCE successfully and gain a first teaching post where she is progressing well. Meanwhile, Caroline successfully applied for a deputy head's post in another school where she is now contributing to many aspects of school improvement, though not involved as a professional mentor.

10 The crowded classroom

Intended learning outcomes

Although a mentor will have their trainees' or NQTs' best interests at heart, the learning welfare and entitlement of pupils remains the core business of the school. What does a mentor do when additional learning support causes professional friction? This case study develops mediation skills and confirms that the beneficial impact on pupils must take precedence in resolving conflict.

Setting the scene

Anisha, who is a newly qualified teacher, is concerned about the quality of the work of the learning mentor who works in her Year 10 mathematics class and calls upon her subject mentor for advice.

Anisha is a very competent teacher who has been timetabled a lower set mathematics group in Year 10 by her head of department who believes that her innovative approaches to teaching and learning, allied to the support from two learning mentors, will offer a great opportunity to raise levels of pupil attainment. Initially, the prediction seems well founded and Anisha reports at the October half term that pupils are engaging better than she anticipated, although she has had to spend time reinforcing skills and knowledge that were not secured in Year 9.

Corridor conversation

A couple of weeks after the half term, Anisha speaks to her subject mentor as they meet on the way to the staff room for morning briefing. During this brief conversation she asks if she is obliged to have learning mentors in her classroom for every mathematics lesson with her Year 10 group. The mentor is taken aback by this enquiry and says that this is something that needs further discussion.

Task one

What do you need to do to ensure that your response is appropriate at this stage?

Getting to the bottom of it

The subject mentor arranges a meeting with Anisha within a few days of their corridor encounter. This reveals Anisha's strong sense that one of the learning mentors is undermining her authority in the classroom. The learning mentor is allocated to three boys who have special educational needs. She has developed a good relationship with these boys over the last year or so and is rather protective towards them, referring to 'her boys' with considerable affection. Although the learning mentor ensures that the boys follow the learning programme provided by Anisha, she often deviates from it on the grounds that she knows the best way for them to learn. Anisha has been very dutiful in her lesson preparation and often provides differentiated work for the boys. Anisha has tried several approaches with the learning mentor but her view is that the learning mentor is determined to adopt her own style because she feels she has the skills to be particularly effective in this curriculum area, given her previous experience as an accounts clerk.

Task two

Identify the issues raised in this discussion. Is the subject mentor the appropriate person to try to resolve this problem or should it be directed to the head of department who is charged with managing mathematics in the school?

Evidence is presented

Anisha has been energised by the subject mentor's tacit support to present evidence of her concerns. She makes photocopies of parts of the boys' work folders and sends copies to both the mentor and the head of department. She annotates the files, drawing attention to the learning mentor's marking and comments. One particular comment is highlighted in bright pink. It reads as follows:

> 'If I was marking this I'd give you a high grade because I know the effort you put into the calculation. Your teacher will have to give it a lower grade because your answer is actually wrong.'

Anisha has annotated this with the following: 'This says it all: the mentor is undermining my role and relationship with this pupil.'

Task three

As is so often the case, this concern is spiralling out of control and the subject mentor realises that not only the head of department but also the assistant headteacher in charge of support staff and the SENCO are likely to have an interest in this matter. The mentor decides to speak with the head of department as a matter of urgency. Decide what these two senior colleagues should do next.

The assistant headteacher becomes involved

Unfortunately, the learning mentor has become increasingly aware of Anisha's disapproval of her ways of working and brings this to the attention of the assistant head teacher, who is responsible for co-ordinating the team of learning mentors and other support staff in the school. The learning mentor is tearful because she feels that her special relationship with the boys, which has influenced their improved attendance and behaviour, is being unfairly challenged by Anisha whom she describes as very aloof and unappreciative of the role of learning mentors. Apparently Anisha has been very assertive in setting learning tasks and has lately insisted that she must mark the boys' work. The trigger to the learning mentor's approach to the assistant head teacher, however, was the institution of a new seating plan that has split up the three boys. Anisha has explained her decision on the grounds of her deployment of peer mentoring within the class to support learning during the 'investigations' section of the scheme of work that is to last until the end of term. The assistant head teacher realises that major professional and personal conflicts are at play and calls the subject mentor and head of department to a meeting to try to resolve the problem. After much discussion and uncertainty, it is agreed that the mentor should speak to Anisha and the learning mentor at a joint meeting.

Task four

Prepare the agenda for this meeting and draft your opening statement.

Barriers removed

The meeting goes surprisingly well. Anisha articulates her concerns professionally and succinctly, focusing on her concern for the pupils' progress. There is hardly a hint of her irritation with the learning mentor. The learning mentor is equally amenable and seems to appreciate the need for these pupils to be more part of the whole class rather than a distinct unit within it.

The subject mentor, although pleased with the tenor of the meeting, and relieved that the underlying friction has not matured into open conflict, recognises that the school has no policy to guide the work of learning mentors. In fact, learning mentors work uniquely in the school and their contribution to pupil welfare and learning is largely predicated on personal relationships with both staff and pupils. This omission is particularly relevant in the case of recently qualified staff who have little experience of working or preparing to work with support staff and who are deeply focused on establishing their professional credibility in the classroom.

Inspection outcomes

The school is in an excellence cluster. HMI has conducted an interim evaluation exercise, as part of a national project, to evaluate the effectiveness of learning mentors in raising the level of pupil attainment and attendance. The inspector, in his brief oral feedback to the school, is complimentary about the work of the learning mentors but does allude to some lack of clarity about their role in core subject areas where the teaching staff see them as 'supplementary rather than complementary' to the pupils' learning. This remark clearly indicates that the support staff policy developed since the Anisha affair has not impacted positively on professional relationships. The inspector refers to the policy document and suggests that one or two key statements need reviewing.

The policy writing team of six volunteer staff included Anisha and the assistant head teacher.

Task five

Consider these statements taken from the policy document. Do they guide the teacher and learning mentor into an appropriate relationship for the benefit of pupils' learning?

- *The classroom teacher is responsible at all times for the management of pupil learning.*

- *The classroom teacher is responsible for the management of all learning resources including support staff.*

End piece

One of the key responsibilities of a mentor is managing staff who contribute not only to a young teacher's professional development but also to the quality of pupil learning. Anisha's reluctance to accept the working methods of the support staff in her classroom points to the importance of lesson planning which maximises learning outcomes through differentiation by input for identified pupils.

But it also points to the changing classroom environment where para-professionals need clear guidance about their professional relationship with the lead educator.

Anisha learned greatly from her experience and has developed some useful protocols for cooperative working.

11 Boys know about foxes

Intended learning outcomes

This case study explores the professional tension created between a mentor and a trainee teacher who reports his concerns about the values and practice of a teacher he has observed. It is about avoiding escalation that in the long term may be destructive to all parties. It raises a fundamental question: should a mentor protect a colleague rather than confront the issued raised? If so, for what greater good?

Setting the scene

Blackstone Community College is a recent amalgamation of two schools, one a former grammar school and the other a secondary modern. The new school is slowly establishing its credibility in the area of the small market town it serves. OFSTED has reported favourably on its progress but did raise some concerns about the quality of teaching and learning with some curriculum areas having a large proportion of teaching that was deemed satisfactory.

Graham's programme for the first week has involved observing experienced practitioners across a wide range of subjects as well as tracking pupils at both Key Stages to gain a sense of the school's curriculum. His mentor has given each lesson observation a particular focus to develop his appreciation of pedagogy and practice. Graham is expected to keep a detailed log of his observations and begin to draw some conclusions about the skills of the effective practitioner and how teachers manage behaviour for learning. Graham has been very dutiful in making notes on the lessons he has observed. He asks if he can use audio equipment to record some parts of lessons and then create a transcript for closer analysis of the teacher-pupil interactions. He feels this would make excellent material for his first college-based assignment. The mentor readily agrees to this small-scale research but clarifies the protocols of securing the permission of the teacher(s) concerned.

At the first tutorial with his mentor Graham says that he has indeed recorded part of a lesson taught by the school's deputy head teacher and has both the recording and a transcript that he wants to discuss with you (as mentor) as he has some concerns about what happened in the lesson.

The mentor asks Graham to indicate his concerns but he seems a little hesitant to share them. He wants the mentor to read the transcript before the conversation continues. The mentor agrees to read it (he is rather impressed with the sheer hard work that has gone into producing the transcript and is quite looking forward to reading it).

Read the transcript and see if you can anticipate the concerns that this trainee teacher is likely to raise with you. You may be slightly surprised that Graham has adopted a playscript format but you attribute this to his background in the performing arts. Graham is a former professional actor who has decided to develop his career prospects by qualifying to teach.

List the concerns you anticipate Graham will raise with you.

Act One Scene 1

Cast: Mr Xavier and pupils: Ismael, Tracey, Peter, Gerry, Rozina, Mumtaz, Michael and Norman

(Mr X enters Room 13 to teach Year 9 English on Tuesday afternoon, first lesson after lunch. He arrives several minutes late and the pupils have already entered the classroom.)

Xavier: Okay, settle down, get your books out and I'll take the register.
Peter: Sir, I haven't got my book. You've got it.
Xavier: Wait, Peter, let me finish the register, then I'll sort you out.

(There are various other minor interruptions before the register is completed. Attendance is 26/31.)

Xavier: Right, Michael, you can move and sit there (*He points to a vacant front desk*) and Tracey you can move to your usual place. Okay, let's look again at Ted Hughes's *Thought Fox*. Ismael, you read it well yesterday. How about another star performance?
Ismael: Me, Sir? Again?
Xavier: Yes, you. I can rely on you to read it with feeling. I think you understand what it is about.

(Ismael reads the poem with much dramatic intent but with little understanding.)

Xavier: Good. Now I know most of you find this a difficult poem but you're bound to get a question on it in the exam, so we'll make sure you've all got good notes to revise from shall we? Ismael, what did we say this poem was about?
Ismael: Writing.
Xavier: Yes, anything else?
Ismael: Can't remember.
Xavier: What about the rest of you? Any ideas?

(There is a disappointing silence.)

Xavier: Tracey? Did you get some notes down yesterday in the lesson?
Tracey: No, Sir, I didn't have time.
Xavier: I don't understand, I gave everyone time and I dictated some key points for everyone.
Tracey: I haven't got them.
Xavier: Well, listen carefully, as I go through it again. You don't want to miss my pearls of wisdom, do you?

(Tracey does not reply.)

Xavier: This poem is a sustained metaphor about the process of creative thought that a poet has, the waiting and the tension before the idea forms in his head and finally enables him to put pen to paper. Okay, let's look at the first few lines carefully. I think a good idea would be to work in groups so that those who have grasped the idea of the poem can share their understanding with those who are struggling.

(Mr Xavier sorts the groups, creating five in total. He then continues.)

When all is said and done, you're set one and you should be able to get this poem faster than any other pupils in Year 9. Right, look at the first four lines and decide in your group anything you do not understand. Jot it down as a question and then we can answer them as a whole-class revision exercise –

(Mr Xavier is interrupted by Peter.)

Peter: Sir, can you tell Gerry to move to his proper group? He's swapped seats with Linda.
Xavier: Gerry, why have you moved? I put you in groups and I expect you to follow my instructions, okay?
Gerry: But, sir, I always end up with Tracey and Rozina – they aren't interested in working, they mess about.
Xavier: Okay, okay, you go back to your proper group and I'll come and check that you're on task, okay?

(Gerry reluctantly returns to his group.)

Tracey: Sir, can we have the windows open? It's really stuffy – it stinks, too, they shouldn't let the packed lunch kids use this room as a canteen.
Xavier: Yes, open a window if you want, then get back to work. You only have a few minutes to get your questions sorted.
Tracey: Sir, the Year 9 council has tried to get the packed lunches moved but nobody's listening.
Xavier: Never mind school council, get the window open, and get your group back to the poem and do it now.
Rozina: Sir?
Xavier: Yes.
Rozina: Sir, could you have a word about the packed lunches? You can get them to do something. They'd listen to you. You're the deputy head.
Xavier: Remind me at the end of the lesson. I'll see what I can do.
Rozina and Tracey: *(with doubting appreciation)* Thanks, Sir.
Xavier: Okay, let's see who has got some good questions for the rest of us. Right, we'll try the girl wonder group by the window. Come on girls, let's have a good question from you.

(There's some mumbling among the group of girls as they can't decide which girl will actually read out the question.)

Xavier: Hurry up, girls. Mumtaz, can you do it please?
Mumtaz: It's not a good question, Sir.
Xavier: It doesn't matter. I want to hear it.
Mumtaz: *(she hesitatingly offers)* 'Why does he use the fox?'
Xavier: That's a great question. I bet some of the boys can guess an answer.

Michael: (*shouts out*) Because they're sly and kill.

Xavier: Don't shout out. Follow the classroom rules and raise your hand, please.

Gerry: (*ignoring the rule*) Because they only go out at night.

Norman: (*ditto*) They are crafty and people hunt them.

Xavier: Do I have to remind you again about the rule? Yes, Ismael what do you want to say?

Ismael: My father shot a fox once because it killed all his hens, and then we had no eggs and no meat for cooking.

Xavier: (*wryly*) Thank you, boys, you have not disappointed me. Boys know about foxes.

> (*Gerry and Norman are pleased with their flippant answers and exchange a knowing look as Ismael offers his answer. Gerry sweeps his forefinger across his throat in a cutting gesture, smiling and Norman nods his understanding. Mr Xavier is unaware of this exchange and moves to another group.*)

Graham is not his usual ebullient self

When Graham joins his mentor for his postponed tutorial a couple of days later, he seems ill at ease and not his normal outgoing self. He is uncertain how to proceed. The mentor tells him that he has read his script and is very interested to know what concerns he wishes to raise.

Graham seems lost for words at first and makes several false starts but eventually he finds his feet and offers the following analysis:

> 'I know this is not an easy class because they're a pretty lively bunch and I know Mr Xavier is really busy as deputy with lots of things to do around school but I was really shocked by what happened in the lesson. The bit I transcribed is only a little bit of the lesson I know but I didn't have time to do any more, but it was pretty typical of what went on.'

Graham pauses at this point to collect his thoughts or perhaps to wait for further guidance from his mentor.

Task two

The mentor senses an emerging problem. What course of action should the mentor follow?

Graham opens up

Graham continues:

> 'When I was in there, it seemed a sort of okay lesson and I made lots of notes but when I listened to the recording I began to hear things and think about things I hadn't noticed during the lesson. I haven't altered the words much but I made it into a scene from a play as a way of distancing myself.'

It is taking some time for Graham to articulate his concerns. He then adds:

'I know Mr Xavier is a very senior member of staff and I am grateful that I can visit different classes and observe teachers but I was unhappy about the way he spoke to the pupils and he seems to have favourites and likes the boys more than the girls. The lesson wasn't really planned either, he just did it and I never saw him check any notes or anything. What I am really unsure about is how to write this up 'cos he said he would be interested to see my analysis of the lesson.'

In this particular case, the mentor chose to redirect Graham in his analysis. He suggested that the close analysis of the language and the interactions between Mr Xavier and the pupils was a rather small sample from which to derive valid conclusions. The mentor accepts that on the face of it, there does seem to be some insensitivity towards the pupils but this could probably be accounted for by the teacher's natural concern to ensure that the pupils had the necessary notes to support their revision and preparation for the forthcoming examination. He further explains that teachers have to work within constraints and that assessment pressures often demand that teachers work in ways that are untypical of their normal teaching style. He realises that Graham is not overly impressed with this explanation and suggests a way forward may be to revisit the transcript with a different purpose. Graham is intrigued by this. The mentor suggests a rewrite of the transcript that demonstrates better practice. In other words, Graham can apply his understanding of effective pedagogy to this brief episode in the lesson and edit the original to create a more acceptable model. This would be both intellectually demanding and provide a good resource to use in his college assignment. Graham accepts this suggestion and the tutorial ends.

A few days later

Mr Xavier speaks to the mentor about Graham. He is checking that he can expect to see Graham's notes on his lesson before he uses them as a basis for his college assignment.

Task three

- *Should the mentor explain why he has set Graham a revised task?*
- *Should the mentor be economical with the truth and fabricate a rationale behind the task Graham is undertaking so that Mr Xavier remains unaware of the concerns that Graham has raised with you?*

The mentor opts for caution

The mentor decides to avoid any professional discomfort with Mr Xavier and assures him that he has already offered some advice to Graham on how to make best use of his lesson observation notes. He thanks Mr Xavier for the time he has given to this trainee and hopes these remarks will remove the necessity for Mr Xavier to be further involved.

The mentor wastes no time in explaining his course of action to Graham and proposes that their dialogue about Mr Xavier's lesson remains confidential to them.

A few days later Graham presents his revised playscript in which the teacher uses different language and clearly treats boys and girls with palpable equal respect. The mentor is rather pleased with Graham's subtle rewrite and actually contemplates sharing it with Mr Xavier.

Task four
- *Has the mentor acted professionally throughout this case study?*
- *If you had been in his position what would you have done differently?*
- *Has the mentor-mentee relationship been strengthened or undermined?*

End piece

The mentor reflected on this difficult situation and incubated a strong sense of guilt at having manipulated the course of events to avoid a potentially embarrassing professional moment. Furthermore, the mentor began to appreciate the challenge of securing consistent training experiences for trainees in which other members of staff model good practice and provide appropriate role models. Set against this thought, the mentor also appreciated the value for trainees of being able to observe a variety of classroom practice and of exercising their critical faculties.

At a meeting of Blackstone's Continuing Professional Development (CPD) group, the mentor stimulated a useful discussion about the roles and responsibilities of staff in respect of ITT within the school. The emerging policy (still in its first draft) has begun to identify key expectations and to establish protocols about observation feedback. As a result, the partnership HEI handbook is likely to have an extended section giving clear advice to trainees on how to deal with situations where they feel moved to comment unfavourably on the practice they have observed.

Reader and tutor notes

Introduction

For each case study, there are notes offering suggestions and guidance on how to achieve best-quality thinking and secure the learning outcomes.

For the tutor working with a group these notes suggest timings and teaching and learning approaches. Many of these will be familiar territory and it is not our intention to patronise the experienced practitioner but rather to offer a few words to act as an *aide-mémoire* to good practice. We have been able to trial many of the case studies with a variety of audiences and the notes reflect our experiences in managing these case studies in real time.

We have learned some important lessons and in the notes we often suggest that the tutor needs to avoid particular pitfalls. The most common are, of course, those situations where the discussion becomes either polarised or animated or both, but becomes tangential or excessively anecdotal. There are clearly tasks that require considerable reflection and others where a speedy response captures the reality of the situation. Obviously, it is at the discretion of the tutor whether or not to invite individual or group engagement with the tasks. We indicate where paired or group work has proved most beneficial. As a general rule, the tutor should adopt a facilitating role throughout each case study and inculcate an ethos where all perceptions and responses are accepted and welcomed. This approach enables trainee mentors to move easily into a positive frame of mind and accelerates the adoption of solution-focused strategies, turning problems into goals and using scaling to identify the next steps in action plans.

Each case study identifies intended learning outcomes but tutors should recognise that professional dialogue among participants often leads to incidental learning. This, on many occasions, enriches the training experience and is to be welcomed, although the usual cautions apply when the discussion becomes too tangential.

For the reader using this book in self-study, we generally advise using the notes only after working through the case studies and engaging with the various tasks. Obviously, individual readers control their own timetable and can indulge in the privilege of skipping over some of the challenges, but this is not recommended as each case study is carefully constructed to elicit and develop mentoring skills and is not amenable to an *ad hoc* approach.

The case studies do not have to be studied in any particular order although the introductory chapter and Chapter 1 are essential reading to appreciate the rationale behind the book and to establish an early definition of the role of mentor.

Picking up the pieces

Overall working time: 2 hours

As a case study designed for those with little or no experience of mentoring trainees, the learning outcomes centre on the following issues:

- preparing for the arrival of trainees and the extent of those involved in the process: the importance of first impressions;
- the advantages and disadvantages of partnership;
- understanding the standards associated with qualified teacher status;
- deployment of teaching staff;
- motivational issues for the trainee;
- an awareness of the different routes into teaching.

Task one (page 14)

For this exercise participants should work in groups. Wherever possible they should be encouraged to draw upon their own experiences, though as trainee mentors these may be limited. Below is a sample Induction Day programme (this is neither prescriptive nor exhaustive). The course tutor may wish to copy this for discussion after participants have presented their own views.

Induction Day programme	
8.30 a.m.	Arrival and coffee with the headteacher and the professional mentor.
9 a.m.	Introduction to the school: standards, expectations and ethos: professional mentor.
9.45 a.m.	Tour of the school: professional mentor.
10.30 a.m.	Coffee in staff room.
11 a.m.	ICT facilities at the school: Head of ICT/e-learning.
11.30 a.m.	Key personnel at the school and organisation of the school: the ITT handbook: professional mentor.
12.15 p.m.	Lunch with headteacher, subject mentors and heads of department in Conference Room (lunch provided).
1.10 p.m.	In subject departments with subject mentors.
3.35 p.m.	Plenary with professional mentor.

A key point here is that trainees should feel comfortable in the school. If they do not they should be given the opportunity to express their concerns during the plenary session and if necessary be placed at an alternative school through liaison with the HEI.

20 minutes.

Task two (page 15)

Within this task the mentors should be able to analyse both the roles and tasks of the mentor. Discussion should focus on the following:

Tutor/critical friend:	Co-ordinate whole school ITT/mentoring provision/programme within school and with the HEI.
Motivator:	Provide individual tutorials.

After this task participants should realise the importance of their role in securing members of the profession for the future. At this critical stage in the case study a potential member of the teaching profession has been lost.

10 minutes.

Task three (page 15)

This task is designed to give the participants an increasing awareness of the whole-school benefits of partnership. Partnership is time-consuming and there is little financial reward or indeed academic accreditation. However, there are tangible advantages. (See: Professional Mentors' perceptions of the contribution of School/HEI Partnerships to Professional Development and School Improvement, published in Vol. 29 Issue 2 of the *Journal of In-Service Education*, 2003.)

The following have been identified as advantages that accrue for secondary schools and departments through involvement in teacher training and mentors should be guided to explore these. The list is by no means exhaustive:

- the encouragement of research and reflective practice within schools;
- the potential of trained mentors adapting their skills for applications beyond teacher training;
- the possibility of securing appointments and reducing recruitment vulnerabilities;
- the engagement with exercising influence on the overall quality of entrants to the teaching profession;
- the involvement in teaching and learning at postgraduate level.

20 minutes.

Task four (page 16)

Mentors should be able to test James's potential to achieve the standards necessary for qualified teacher status. They should explore why James withdrew from the PGCE course. This case study has proved particularly successful when a member of the training team has taken on the role of James and course participants have been the interviewing committee.

25 minutes.

Task five (page 16)

Mentors should understand their role in its widest sense. For the trainer it may be useful if course delegates refer back to Task three at this stage. The theoretical advantages of partnership have been identified in that task but how are these desired advantages to be put into practice within the parameters of the situation in terms of the personnel in the department and the needs of the school?

Course participants should consider not only the teaching staff available to contribute to James's professional needs, but also the growing group of para-professionals and support staff. For example, as administrative tasks are removed from the portfolio of teachers how does James engage reprographic and secretarial staff to enhance his development as a teacher?

15 minutes.

Task six (page 17)

Coach/trainer:	Give feedback, lead reviews, evaluate trainee performance and competence, write reports, complete documentation, etc.
Assessor:	Observe trainee teaching.

The above roles and tasks of the mentor may prove helpful in providing discussion:
Reflection is the key issue to any profession that wants to progress. A critical role of the mentor is to encourage and develop a reflective approach by the trainee. Reflective practice is increasingly used as both an educational philosophy and also as a development tool in other professions (e.g. medicine) and in other spheres of education. It may be said that the underlying philosophy of teaching is that of *reflective practice*.

The following suggestions may help to explain the nature of reflective practice and could be adopted and adapted for use by mentors in the process of lesson feedback.

- What was I trying to achieve?
- Why did I act as I did?
- What were the consequences of my actions for my students and my colleagues?
- How did I feel about this experience when it was happening?
- How did the students feel about it?
- How do I know how the students felt about it?
- What factors influenced my decisions and actions?
- What knowledge affected my decisions and actions?

20 minutes.

Final reflections

The tutor might want to reproduce the following points as a handout for participants to take away with them or to reflect upon informally before bringing everyone together in a plenary to summarise the key outcomes.

- Consider the number of staff that have had an input into James' training.
- How have they contributed to the training process?
- The word 'vitality' is used in the end piece. How would mentors define the use of this word?
- What were the key ingredients in the mentoring programme that motivated James after his initial unfortunate experiences on the PGCE course?
- How has the school actually benefited from the training experience?

Jennifer Eccles: gifted and talented but plans on a postcard

Overall working time: 2 hours

The learning outcomes focus on:

- the importance of meeting all the standards for QTS;
- the nature of evidence to support attainment of a particular standard;
- the responsibility to record accurately progress towards the attainment of a standard.

Task one (page 20)

Most participants engage in this task with great enthusiasm because they feel very comfortable offering a critique of a trainee teacher's planning. Most teachers and trainee mentors have considerable expertise in this area and are happy to display their knowledge of appropriate pedagogical practice. It is probably best to complete the lesson plan on an individual basis, allowing six or seven minutes for the scripting of observations. A paired exchange can then follow. The discussion is usually animated. The tutor can do a simple survey to assess the audience's view of Jennifer's planning by asking participants to classify the lesson plan as unsatisfactory, satisfactory or good.

6–8 minutes.

Task two (page 22)

Allow a good ten minutes for this writing, that should be done as a paired activity. The tutor should then invite these opening paragraphs to be shared with the whole group. Of course, depending on the number of participants it may not be possible to hear all the versions. It would be very surprising if there were not a wide range of approaches that reflect the deep-seated values and beliefs of practising teachers. Some authors are not prepared to support Jennifer's application, believing she has yet to attain the standard of lesson planning required. Others structure their paragraph so that the recipient would read between the lines and gain a sense of some concern. A few may choose to write a bland paragraph that merely introduces the reference. The post-reading aloud session also encourages a worthwhile debate about the confidentiality of references. But fundamentally, the discussion should focus on the quality of the evidence that the mentor has of Jennifer's progress towards meeting the QTS standard. The tutor might want to pose one or two questions to conclude the session:

- Is there an inevitable conflict in the role of mentor as coach and assessor?
- Should a mentor be charged with the sole responsibility of writing a reference or should this be a co-ordinated activity managed by the Professional Mentor so that other teachers contribute?

Spend as much time as you see fit on this discussion.

Task three (page 22)

Conduct a open discussion to answer the question posed.

10–15 minutes.

Task four (page 24)

Some participants may want to comment on Jennifer's rather churlish note. Do not allow this to deflect from the task. The key learning point is to address the question: how does a mentor balance the quality of lesson planning documentation against the quality of lesson delivery?

The prompts in the case study itself should direct discussion well enough but the tutor should ensure that each of the prompts is addressed. On some occasions, the discussion has focused readily on bullet points 3 and 4. The tutor may find it useful during this discussion session to circulate around the groups, eavesdropping and also acting as an *agent provocateur*. When we used this case study with a group of trainee mentors, there was considerable reaction to our proposal that Jennifer would actually fail her PGCE/QTS if her lesson planning stayed at its current level. This produced cries of anguish from the audience who argued that she had so much potential that this must outweigh her cavalier attitude to planning, recording and reporting. Others argued, with some justification no doubt, that the reality of her first job would cause her to rethink and be compelled into a more professional approach. The argument was that the culture and expectations in schools nowadays are such that teachers are far better at planning and that performance management, etc., has generated the need for solid evidence of professional activity. Another ploy was to suggest that the standards for QTS (even if you are familiar with the detail contained in the accompanying handbook) are still wide open to personal interpretation and that ITT providers are essentially happy to take the placement school's assessment as *bona fide* and rarely challenge it.

20–25 minutes.

Final reflections

This case study probably raises more questions than answers but a neat way to bring it to a conclusion is to ask each participant to identify what they have learned from working through it. We recommend that this should be a formal writing exercise in professional reflection.

After this the tutor may wish to share some of these comments, which emerged from other trainee mentors who worked on this case study.

'I am going to talk to the Professional Mentor about the protocols for writing references.'

'At the next meeting with the University tutors the agenda must be about the assessment processes we use.'

'There needs to be closer liaison between first and second placement schools.'

'I don't see how we can accurately comment on a trainee's potential – this is a subjective value judgement.'

'I don't care what anyone else said during the session: the heart of good teaching is planning and preparation and that's what I have always concentrated on with my trainees.'

The ambitious fast-tracker

Overall working time: 2 hours

The intended learning outcomes for this case study centre around the following issues:

- an understanding of the fast track programme;
- trainees make occasional unreasonable demands;
- confidentiality among trainees privileged to particular information;
- the management of conflict within the school as a result of the actions of a trainee and ensuring that positive relationships within the school are maintained.

Task one (page 26)

Within this task course members should be able to discuss where their loyalties lie. There is a need to work closely with all stakeholders in the partnership but there is also the need to be protective and supportive of the department. The point should be highlighted that the core business of the school is teaching and learning and not the training of teachers. However, the participation in partnership as a structured by-product can enhance teaching and learning. Indeed the *raison d'être* of the school may prove to be a focal point for participants to discuss within this task. The trainer will want also to emphasise the benefits of partnership.

15 minutes.

Task two (page 27)

In order for mentors to be involved in the training of fast-track trainees there is a need to be aware of the facets of the scheme associated with school management and leadership. Depending upon the experience of the group that is training, the following suggestions may be appropriate:

- the work of the senior leadership team – attendance at SLT meetings;
- the tasks of a senior manager – shadowing a deputy head teacher for the day;
- the role of the middle leader – attendance at curriculum planning meetings.

As the case study evolves, the associated problems of inclusion of the fast-track trainee will become apparent.

20 minutes.

Task three (page 28)

The course tutor may like to consider the parameters of the role of the Professional Mentor. Key questions that may arise from this task include:

- Is the subject mentor correct to involve the Professional Mentor on this issue? Is this threatening the credibility of the subject mentor?
- How would you suggest that David improves his lesson plan? As an ICT specialist should the subject mentor have a sample lesson plan available?
- How should the Professional Mentor conclude the meeting with David? Again, there is the need to maintain the credibility of the subject mentor.

15 minutes.

Task four (page 29)

The purpose of this task is to examine the skills of the mentor as mediator and motivator. There has been a threat to the subject mentor but she is still a key player in the partner-ship. For the purposes of training it is suggested that the meeting between the department, the subject mentor and the Professional Mentor could be enacted. Participants may like to take on a variety of roles that reflect the personalities that exist in any secondary school department.

20 minutes.

Task five (page 30)

Confidentiality can be a major issue. Participants must decide exactly how far David has overstepped the mark. His actions, especially in the light of his previous attitude, are a cause for concern and the experienced head of year and his team will be looking to the mentor to take appropriate action. There are a number of possibilities open to the mentor.

- Does the Professional Mentor inform the college of David's actions?
- Does the Professional Mentor insist that David leaves the school completely as he has alienated staff to such an extent that his presence in school will prove untenable?
- Is a short-term suspension appropriate?

The actual decision taken is revealed as the case study develops but it should be emphasised by the tutor that this is not the only route open to the mentor. As the case study unfolds it proves an effective decision.

10 minutes.

Task six (page 31)

References are confidential documents. After writing the reference, participants may like to consider the merits and demerits of sharing the reference with David. Emphasis should be placed on referring to the standards for QTS that are highlighted in the task: 1.3, 1.5, 1.6 and 3.1.4. A further exercise could be for participants to exchange references and analyse critically the references of other groups.

20 minutes.

Final reflections

The tutor might want to reproduce the following questions as a handout for participants to take away with them or to reflect upon informally before bringing everyone together in a plenary to summarise the key outcomes.

- How do mentors manage the fast-track programme, to avoid divisiveness?
- Where do the mentors' loyalties lie when there is a challenge to the organisation from trainees?
- How do mentors ensure confidentiality when trainees are placed in privileged positions?

Eleanor Rigby: rings on her fingers and bells on her toes

Overall working time: 2 hours

The intended learning outcomes centre around these issues:

- an awareness of the need to support the ethos and traditions of the school at a time of challenge;
- an ability to empathise with the less experienced subject mentor and to provide appropriate support as they develop their own skills;
- the concept of partnership – when and how to involve the HEI;
- the ability to assess trainees against the following standards:

1.3 They demonstrate and promote positive values, attitudes and behaviour that they expect from pupils.
1.5 They can contribute to and share responsibility in the corporate life of the school.
1.7 They are able to improve their own teaching, by evaluating it, learning from the effective practice of others and from evidence. They are motivated and able to take increasing responsibility for their own professional development.

Task one (page 34)

Within this case study Professional Mentors are faced with conflict from the onset of the placement. Participants should consider how they will approach Eleanor in order to maintain standards in the school. The question about involvement of the college suggests that the college has either not adequately prepared Eleanor for the practice in terms of professional values and practice or that Eleanor has ignored the advice that is given.

10 minutes.

Task two (page 35)

In the first instance discussion may centre upon whether it was appropriate for the Professional Mentor to meet Eleanor alone. The following questions could be raised by the course leader:

- Was the credibility of the subject mentor undermined?
- Did the Professional Mentor show an understanding of the difficulties of the subject mentor?
- Have the skills of the subject mentor been enhanced by the decisions of the Professional Mentor?

Participants may like to consider how well they have met these learning outcomes. The course tutor may decide to ask participants whether or not the professional mentor has used the skills of compromise, professionalism and maintained respect.

10 minutes.

Task three (page 36)

Course tutors should issue copies of Eleanor's notes. Participants should be prepared for questions and points that Eleanor may raise and how she may react. For example:

- Am I going to be asked to leave the school/course?
- How will my future be affected?
- The school has not provided appropriate guidance.
- I have been the subject of discrimination from day one.
- What is going to happen to me at the end of this meeting?

20 minutes.

Task four (page 38)

Invite participants to note down *how* they have learned during this case study. We have been fascinated by the fact that some participants speak of identification and others of 'helicoptering' above the episodes – both have merit as ways of learning.

1 Decide what the professional mentor and the subject mentor have learned from Eleanor's practice taking into account the following:

- learning is reflective;
- learning is experiential;
- learning is developmental.

2 How could professional mentors change their approach to mentoring from their experience with Eleanor?

3 How would the subject mentor change her approach to mentoring?

It may be helpful to consider which of the following roles and tasks you have performed in this case study.

The role of the mentor	The tasks of the mentor
Role model	Be observed teaching, organise observation of other experienced teachers.
Coach/trainer	Give feedback, lead reviews, evaluate trainee performance and competence, write reports, complete documentation, etc.
Assessor	Observe trainee teaching.
Confidant(e)/advisor	Liaise with school management (e.g. CPD co-ordinator; heads of department, etc.), devise teaching timetable for trainee.
Tutor/critical friend	Co-ordinate whole school ITT/mentoring provision/ programme.
Protector/negotiator	Liaise with ITT provider (HEIs).
Ambassador	Integrate ITT into whole school improvement plan.
Facilitator	Attend mentor training.
Motivator	Provide individual tutorials.
Counsellor/advisor	Ensure trainee's health and safety.

The new mentor: a baptism of fire

Overall working time: 2 hours

The intended learning outcomes from this case study centre around the following issues:

- developing working relationships in difficult circumstances and with an NQT who is less than co-operative;
- communication skills – with both the NQT and senior line managers;
- decision-making skills – when is it appropriate to involve others in the mentoring process?
- the parameters of the role of the professional mentor.

Task one (page 40)

In the same way that the first day is vital for initial teacher training students, an effective Induction Day is required for NQTs. In this task it is appropriate that the tutor should provide guidelines as to what is required for such a day. It is also pertinent for course members to ask the question, 'If I were new to a school what would I benefit from knowing from the first day?' The following questions will help delegates concentrate on requirements:

- What will the NQT expect from the mentor?
- How will the NQT be assessed?
- Is there a formalised in-house induction programme?
- How will the Career Entry Development Profile be used?
- How are ICT facilities accessed?

It is also appropriate to involve other key staff in the process of induction, preferably on a day before the start of the new term. For example, the ICT co-ordinator may be able to log the NQTs on to the system and the presence of the headteacher is also desirable. A human touch is to organise induction on the basis of a continental day followed by lunch at an appropriate venue off-site.

20 minutes.

Task two (page 41)

It is important when giving feedback from lesson observations that the mentor is well prepared. This exercise could be approached by suggesting that the mentor raises questions for Jeremy to answer in order to allow him to reflect. For example, the mentor may ask, 'What did the pupils learn in this lesson?' or 'How was the pupils' knowledge enhanced by this lesson?' or 'How do you know the pupils learnt?'

The mentor's role is to develop the reflective practitioner and a good rule of thumb for feedback is that the NQT should speak for 70 per cent of the time.

For the purpose of this task it may be appropriate for delegates to take on the role of the mentor and Jeremy. The possibilities for raising a challenge for the mentor are endless. It is also interesting to note that the mentor's subsequent memo to Jeremy appropriately highlights the areas of development that are required as a result of the observation: however, is the memo the best form of communication? Is the written form a 'get out?'

20 minutes.

Task three (page 44)

This is a particularly challenging situation for the mentor. His credibility is at stake with both the NQTs and the remainder of the staff. The mentor has to decide whether he feels sufficiently confident to deal with the situation in isolation or he needs to involve senior management within the school. Acting independently may lead to repercussions; involving others may lead to a complete loss of face, particularly with Jeremy. As the case study develops, the mentor's decision to act alone proves to be successful in the short term, but do the participants share in the approval of this action? The possibilities for disagreement are immense and the views of course members should provide an interesting stage for debate.

15 minutes.

Task four (page 45)

This task enables the mentor to engage in positive feedback. However, the mentor should still question Jeremy's methods, in particular his apparent favouritism of boys and how this lesson developed compared with the previous observation of the Year 8 class. The intention is to allow the NQT to develop his practice by questioning his actions.

15 minutes.

Task five (page 46)

Within this task it is necessary for the mentor to justify his actions. The role of the mentor is vital as a quality assurance mechanism in the induction year. If failures occur the position of the mentor may be called into question. The mentor must be able to justify all decisions and show how support has been implemented to address problems. Within this case study the mentor is called upon to justify his actions. The course leader may like to raise the following questions to facilitate discussion:

- Was the mentor's decision not to involve others after the incident in the staff room the correct one?
- Did the mentor follow procedures after his initial concerns over the Year 8 lesson observation?
- Is the senior management team guilty of failing to implement its duty of care with the new mentor?

20 minutes.

Final reflections

The tutor might want to reproduce the following questions and points as a handout for participants to take away with them or to reflect upon informally before bringing everyone together in a plenary to summarise the key outcomes.

- As mentors, when and how do we involve others in the mentoring process, particularly when inexperienced?
- How do mentors assist a teacher who is competent in certain areas to address a lack of skills in other areas?
- The realisation of the need to work within the standards for QTS and the provision of evidence that these standards are being met.

The language of life

Overall working time: 2 hours

The intended learning outcomes centre around these issues:

- the tension between the role of mentor as provider of professional subject/pastoral support and as headteacher's representative in a disciplinary procedure;
- the skill profile required to succeed in mentoring in both subject and pastoral domains.

Task one (page 49)

Spend about five or six minutes on this task. Take verbal responses only and perhaps capture the general consensus on a flipchart.

Task two (page 49)

Discussion should focus on the conventions and protocols that apply. For example, would a more human touch have been to speak to Peter and then confirm the content of the conversation by letter? A paired discussion is advised here.

5–6 minutes.

Task three (page 50)

At this stage in the case study the mentor is facing an *increasing* level of challenge. The focus moves inexorably to some key issues that imperil the professional wellbeing of all concerned. The subject mentor might feel isolated and under pressure. Would reference to the Professional Mentor be appropriate?

The subject mentor now has to establish the rules of confidentiality that apply to this meeting. This is always a difficult area and is worth some considerable discussion. Peter seems determined to sort things out for himself. Could a subject mentor instruct Peter not to do so and speak with the delegated responsibility of the headteacher? Tutors might allocate discussion to groups of four and ask each group to explore one of the three bullet points. Each group should prepare a brief summary of their thinking to report back in a plenary.

15–20 minutes.

Task four (page 51)

In asking the trainee mentors to prepare to respond to Peter's questions, the tutor may again opt to divide responsibility on a group basis. Some groups may well suggest other concerns that Peter has at this juncture. In one sense it is not necessary to share answers to all these questions publicly but it is important to draw out the concept of the effective mentor seeing things from the mentee's perspective and of being proactive in anticipating the likely challenges. Question 5 can stimulate a fascinating discussion about the recording of the meeting: is it an agreed set of minutes or is each party to offer their own version?

Another interesting technique is to use the miracle question: Imagine that a magic wand is waved over this situation what would be the perfect solution?

20–25 minutes.

An optional approach

This case study has proved particularly successful when a member of the training team has taken on the role of Peter Baggley and a course delegate has taken on the role of mentor. Other delegates can assist the mentor in the preparation for this meeting while another trainer could take the union representative role. Carefully controlled by the trainer, the unexpected nature/uncertainty of such meetings can be carefully managed. For example, in one scenario Peter Baggley could offer his resignation; in another he could accuse the school and his mentor of a lack of professionalism and duty of care. Using forum theatre has also proved very powerful in drawing out the role of mentor.

Final reflections

The tutor might want to reproduce the following questions as a handout for participants to take away with them or to reflect upon informally before bringing everyone together in a plenary to summarise the key outcomes.

The role of mentor is rarely circumscribed by a job specification and a mentor can expect to operate outside it. Indeed, personal qualities are as important as professional competences.

- Did the headteacher manage this incident in a sensitive way by delegating responsibility to the mentor?
- Should the mentor have anticipated the likelihood of Peter acting inappropriately, given the early indications of his view of the role of teacher and the manner in which he secured acceptable classroom behaviour?
- Was it appropriate for Peter to be on dinner queue duty (a voluntary activity) in an unsupervised capacity?
- How should SW be dealt with by the school?
- Peter's credibility and professional standing could be greatly compromised by the in-school publicity surrounding this incident. What is the subject mentor's role in minimising this?
- Should Peter receive a formal verbal warning about his conduct?
- What training and support should Peter receive to manage challenging pupil behaviour? Anger management?
- Would you, as subject mentor, broker a meeting between SW and Peter?

Carrie Anne: Oh yes I will, oh no I won't

Overall working time: 2 hours

The intended learning outcomes centre around these issues:

- professionalism: the role of the mentor in ensuring the credibility of procedures in teaching;
- an ability to develop trainees to their full potential and prepare them for securing their first teaching post;
- an understanding of conflict and tension between the role of mentor and support for the trainee and the wellbeing of the profession;
- the ability to take difficult decisions based on personal beliefs.

Task one (page 53)

The trainer should concentrate on the fact that for the second practice the development of trainees arriving in schools will vary. Clearly Carrie Anne has the makings of a good teacher and an appropriate programme for development should be formulated. Mentors need to appreciate that differentiated programmes are required for each trainee and that a needs analysis is no easy task. Discussion within this task should concentrate on a somewhat accelerated programme in order that Carrie Anne's full potential is realised.

10 minutes.

Task two (page 54)

By the end of this task participants should have formulated the ingredients of a session to enhance trainees' awareness of what schools look for in applications. The focus of discussion should be on procedures that schools take after making appointments and the protocol involved in securing posts. The fact that Carrie Anne does not attend the session will be of paramount significance as this case study develops.

20 minutes.

Task three (page 54)

The task is designed to allow mentors to balance their previous experiences of a trainee with current behaviour. Clearly the mentor will have been taken by surprise by the content of Carrie Anne's note. Any form of non-compliance could have disastrous results at a later stage in the practice. The course leader should point this out as participants embark upon the activity. It would also be pertinent to ask how non-compliance might prejudice the future relationship between mentor and trainee as, at this stage, delegates are not aware how the case study will evolve.

20 minutes.

Task four (page 56)

After her absence and appointment to the post, however, Carrie Anne is now showing a less than professional approach to teaching. The participants should be aware that they do not act in isolation. The concept of partnership is of vital importance. The focus of development now moves to involvement of the college and the need to work in harmony for the benefit of all trainees now and in the future.

15 minutes.

Task five (page 56)

Discussion should centre on the conventions and protocols that apply. In addition to the task, the course tutor may like to raise the following points to enhance discussion:

- How would your school react if a member of staff was 'poached' by another school?
- Is your own professionalism threatened by complying with Carrie Anne's request?
- We live in a free market economy, don't we?

10 minutes.

Task six (page 57)

Members of the course take on the roles of the Professional Mentor, subject mentor and Carrie Anne. This can lead to an interesting exchange of opinions. The end piece explains what really happened but will the meeting reflect this? Certain groups may take an unadventurous approach while others will display their resentment at the threat to their professionalism. In one training session, considerable debate was generated when a participant playing the role of Carrie Anne made a very articulate case for putting her welfare before that of all others. She argued her greatest obligation was to self. On another occasion it was argued that a handshake confirming and accepting the offer of a post was a legally binding contract!

15 minutes.

Final reflections

The tutor might want to reproduce the following questions as a handout for participants to take away with them or to reflect upon informally before bringing everyone together in a plenary to summarise the key outcomes.

- As mentors, how do we weight competence in pedagogical practice and the need for professionalism?
- Where do mentors' responsibilities end with respect to Standard 1.8: 'They are aware of, and work within, the statutory frameworks relating to teachers' responsibilities'?
- What are the key issues for the mentor in terms of providing references that are an honest reflection of the trainee's ability to meet all the standards?

Not-so-sweet Caroline

Overall working time: 2 hours

The intended learning outcomes from this case study centre around the following issues:

- the role of the mentor in developing a relationship with the trainee and the partnership university;
- the mentor as observer and the ability to give meaningful feedback after lesson observations;
- relating the theory of the standards for qualified teacher status with practice in the classroom;
- issues of professionalism.

Task one (page 60)

Discussion should focus on the wider issues involved in partnership. How, as a structured by-product, can partnership contribute to whole school improvement? The following points should prove helpful to the tutor:

- the encouragement of research and reflective practice within schools;
- the potential of trained mentors adapting their skills for applications beyond teacher training;

- the possibility of securing appointments and reducing recruitment vulnerabilities;
- the engagement with exercising influence on the overall quality of entrants to the teaching profession;
- the involvement in teaching and learning at postgraduate level for both teaching and non-teaching staff.

15 minutes.

Task two (page 61)

For observations to be successful it is essential for the observer to consider the context of the lesson. Has Caroline actually done this? It is doubtful whether or not Caroline did consider the essential preparatory questions that the trainee mentors are working with.

A study of a failing mentor can prove to be an effective tool for developing the new mentor. Task two will emphasise the shortcomings of the mentor and the power that they have to make or break the trainee.

15 minutes.

Task three (page 62)

At this point in the case study there is evidence of a threat to the mentor-trainee relationship. Course participants need to be aware that mentoring is based on mutual trust and respect. Discussion should lead on from Task two, highlighting that the process of feedback from lesson observations is crucial and that Caroline's methods threaten not only the relationship between her and the trainee but also the relationship between mentor and department and school and university.

The following points should be emphasised at the conclusion of this task. Effective feedback should be:

- unbiased – recognising the positive and the negative (always start and end with a positive);
- based upon foci agreed before the lesson;
- without assumption – comment only on what has been observed;
- uninterrupted;
- in sympathy with the trainee's stage of development.

20 minutes.

Task four (page 63)

The components for effective lesson observations are outlined. Course participants should be able to analyse whether or not these components have been implemented in Caroline's feedback.

The conflict that has arisen threatens the whole nature of the partnership. For the trainee mentors it may be useful to return to Task one, the benefits of partnership. Further discussion could centre on how these benefits are being negated by Caroline's actions.

10 minutes.

Task five (page 64)

There is an obvious issue of transparency here. Course tutors need to make the point that, despite what may have occurred and despite personal feelings, there must be mutual respect and an atmosphere of openness if partnerships are to succeed for the benefit of all involved. Questions could be raised about the concept of professionalism.

15 minutes.

Task six (page 65)

A very successful approach to this task is to allow participants individual time to draft answers to the three questions. Then, the tutor, is 'hot seated' as Caroline and answers any question put to her by the delegates – it's fun and the tutor can bring out some key learning points. It's not a methodology for everyone but a stimulating exercise when done well and with purpose.

25 minutes.

Final reflections

The tutor might want to reproduce the following questions as a handout for participants to take away with them or to reflect upon informally before bringing everyone together in a plenary to summarise the key outcomes.

By the end of this case study trainee mentors should be able to consider the following questions:

- What are the attributes required for successful mentoring?
- How would you differentiate between the role of the mentor and the tasks of the mentor?
- What are the key issues in lesson observation and how should these be related to the standards for qualified teacher status?

The crowded classroom

Overall working time: two hours

The learning outcome focuses on:

- the management of a teacher's relationship with other professionals who support pupil learning.

Task one (page 66)

This task is very much a warm-up activity to get participants talking. It is probably best to invite informal paired discussion in response to this question. If the participants do not readily engage, then these additional points could be highlighted on a flipchart or OHT:

- Has the school got a clear policy on in-class support?
- Has the learning mentor got a specific responsibility to certain pupils?

- Has someone in school got specific responsibility for the management of learning mentors?
- What factors could have led to Anisha raising this question with her mentor?

5–6 minutes.

Task two (page 67)

This question seeks to clarify where the mentor's responsibilities lie. It is not unreasonable for Anisha to have spoken to her mentor about her concerns and the school has worked hard to develop mentoring and coaching as part of its CPD programme. It is motivated not only to maintain and raise standards of pupil attainment but also to retain the staff it has worked so hard to recruit. Allow about five minutes for paired discussion.

5–6 minutes.

Task three (page 67)

Here, the mentor has decided that the matter requires the intervention and support of several colleagues and is proactive in securing their involvement in a planned way rather than letting the matter spiral into the confusion of mixed messages. This is not an untypical problem in schools where people management is complicated by the portfolio of responsibilities that sit in a matrix management model.

Divide participants into two groups. The first group should explore what the assistant head teacher's course of action should be; the second group should identify the scope of SENCO's involvement at this stage.

At some point the tutor should pose the question: Does the complex nature of this situation with several key stakeholders ultimately undermine the mentor's status?

10 minutes.

Task four (page 68)

This is a positive management move to bring the central players together under the stewardship of the mentor. However, this will not be an easy meeting. Organise the participants into small groups and ask them to draft some guidelines for the conduct of the meeting. To help each group, you may want to draw their attention to these questions:

- What is the area of tension?
- Who is ultimately responsible for the quality of teaching and learning in the classroom?
- What is the basis of a professional relationship between a class teacher and a learning mentor?
- Although the concern is to ease the tension between Anisha and the learning mentor, what is the fundamental purpose behind the meeting?

Another way to get the groups thinking is to try the miracle question technique. Imagine a fairy godmother could wave her wand over this situation and produce, at your bidding, the perfect solution. Describe this perfect solution.

Use your discretion about how much time to allocate to this task. The miracle question approach can produce a surprisingly detailed and extensive response, with participants drafting some key ideas of policy and practice.

Task five (page 68)

If the participants are engaging well, the tutor might want to push them into drafting some statements for a school policy on best practice in the deployment of additional support in the classroom. To stimulate discussion, try offering this statement: 'The classroom teacher is responsible at all times for the management of pupil learning and responsible for the management of all learning resources including support staff.' To what extent do you agree with this?

Final reflections

This case study placed the mentor in a difficult position. The mentor could not escape some professional responsibility to Anisha but what is clear as the narrative unfolds is that the mentor does not have a defined line manager relationship with Anisha. So, if a mentor is perceived as a coach and critical friend, should they be expected to resolve conflicts of this kind without the authority of managerial status?

Boys know about foxes

Overall working time: 2 hours

The intended learning outcomes centre on:

- building a trainee teacher's confidence and competence in lesson observation of experienced practitioners;
- sustaining professional relationships when practitioner competence is challenged.

Task one (page 71)

Participants could act the transcript to bring the text alive. They may appreciate a quick private read through before the group reading. The tutor should take on the role of the deputy head teacher, enabling key emphases to be made in the interaction with the pupils. The participants should then be guided to work in pairs to identify what they think Graham's five concerns will be.

30 minutes.

The tutor should summarise/collect these concerns on a flipchart.

6–7 minutes.

Task two (page 73)

Allow three or four minutes' personal reflection. Then ask: What are the options for the mentor? Possible answers include:

- the mentor could park these concerns and offer to come back to Graham once he has reflected further;
- the mentor could invite Graham to say more but would probably need to offer assurances about confidentiality;

- the mentor could suggest that Graham's interpretation may be overly critical and offer alternative insights;
- the mentor could help Graham find a solution to the problem by exploring the steps towards converting this problem into a goal;
- the mentor might adopt a counsellor role to ease Graham's discomfort.

The tutor may want to stimulate discussion by offering these mentor actions but this will depend on the level of engagement among the participants. The key issue to raise is the mentor's professional responsibility to Graham versus his responsibility to the deputy head teacher.

10 minutes.

Task three (page 74)

- Should the mentor explain why he has set Graham a revised task?
- Should the mentor be economical with the truth and fabricate a rationale behind the task Graham is undertaking so that Mr Xavier remains unaware of the concerns that Graham has raised with you?

To energise the session, work through the first question as a plenary and allow some open and fairly unstructured debate. Is this revised task a professionally appropriate one?

The second question can be responded to in paired discussion. It frequently leads to very polarised viewpoints among participants. There is merit, of course, in either path the mentor chooses to take but some participants can be adamant that in not sharing Graham's concerns with Mr Xavier, the mentor is failing in his professional duty. As tutor, it is worth adopting a neutral stance at this juncture and allowing the debate to simmer.

10 minutes.

Task four (page 75)

The participants may have already indicated some dislike/disapproval of the way the mentor in this scenario has acted. This final task is an opportunity to clarify the key values and beliefs that underpin professional responsibilities in participants' minds. It should come as no surprise that practitioners are often faced with ethical dilemmas and need to manage and consider the welfare of more than one colleague.

Display the folllowing questions and invite each participant to draft a written response.

- Has the mentor acted professionally throughout this challenging moment?
- If you had been the mentor what would you have done differently?
- Has the relationship between Graham and his mentor been enhanced or weakened by the unfolding events?

To encourage some speedy thinking, and responses to these questions why not use a scaling approach. A five point scale for bullet points 1 and 2 works really well and then invite other solutions/opinions in answer to bullet point 2.

10 minutes.

Final reflections

It is important that trainee teachers are able to work with teachers who model good practice. They can learn so much from successful classroom practitioners. The mentor has to exercise careful judgement so that the trainee is safeguarded from the influences of teachers whose practice is not of the required standard. In this case study, the mentor was faced with a considerable dilemma in that a senior colleague's practice raised concerns for the trainee. The mentor felt unable to deal with these other than by sidestepping them and opting for a solution that avoided professional discomfort with the deputy head teacher and encouraged the trainee to change the problem into a worthwhile goal.

You may be highly critical of this mentor and be utterly convinced that you would have acted in a totally different way. You may have some sympathy for the mentor's dilemma and recognise that the adopted course of action was a reasonable resolution to the challenge. Your final reflection, however, should be about Graham Barlow. What conclusion would he draw from this experience?

Further reading

Anderson, L. (1995) Conceptions of Partnership in school-centred initial teacher training in Bines, H. and Welton, J. (eds) *Managing Partnership in Teacher Training and Development*. London: Routledge.

Barnes, S. and Bennett, N. (2001) Promoting a Culture of Collaboration through Continuing Professional Development, *Management in Education*, Vol 15 Issue No 5

Blum, P. (2001) *A Teacher's Guide to Anger Management*. London: Routledge Falmer

Boyd, P. (2002) Rose tinted education? The benefits for teachers of ITT in secondary schools. *Journal of In-Service Education*, Vol 28 Issue 2

Bubb, S. and Earley, P. (2004) *Leading and Managing Continuing Professional Development*. London: Paul Chapman Publishing

Butler, S. and Geeson, J. (2002) Why Everyone Needs Mentoring. *Secondary English Magazine*, Vol 5 Issue 3

Carroll, C. and Simco, N. (2001) *Succeeding as an Induction Tutor.* Exeter: Learning Matters

Child, A. and Merrill, S. (2002) Making the Most of ITT (Initial Teacher Training), *Professional Development Today*, Vol 5 Issue 2, Spring 2002

Child, A. and Merrill, S. (2003) Changing the professional landscape through mentoring: school/university partnering in the UK, in Kochan, F. and Pascarelli, J. (Eds), *Global perspectives on mentoring: transforming contexts, communities and cultures*. Information Age Publishing, Greenwich, Connecticut

Child, A. and Merrill, S. (2003) Professional mentors' perceptions of the contribution of school/HEI partnerships to professional development and school improvement. *Journal of In-Service Education*. Vol 29 Issue 2

Department for Education in England (DFE) (1992), *Circular 9/92: Initial Teacher Training (secondary phase)*. London

Department for Education and Skills (DfES). (2002) *Qualifying to teach: professional standards for qualified teacher status and requirements for initial teacher training*. London

Dunn, E. and Bennett, N. (1997) Mentoring Processes in School-based Training, *British Education Research Journal*, 23

Holmes, E., (1999) *Handbook for New Qualified Teachers*, London: HMSO

Jones, M., (2002) Qualified to become good teachers: a case study of ten newly qualified teachers during their year of induction. *Journal of In-service Education*, Vol 28 Issue 3

Jones, M. (2001b) Mentors' perceptions of their roles. *Journal of Education for Teaching*. Vol 27 Issue 1

Kabra, K. (2002), *From Initial Teacher Training to a Learning Community*, in Professional Development Today, Autumn 2002 , Vol 5 Issue 3

Kerry, T. and Mayes, S. (1995) *Issues in Mentoring*. London: Routledge

McIntyre, D. and Hagger, H (Eds.) (1996) *Mentors in Schools*. London: David Fulton

Maynard, T. and Furlong, J. (1995) Learning to teach and models of mentoring. In T. Kerry and A. Shelton Mayes (Eds) *Issues in Mentoring*. London: Open University Press

Tomlinson. P. (1995) *Understanding Mentoring*. Buckingham, UK: Open University Press

Veenman, S. De Laat, H. and Staring, C. (1998) Evaluation of a Coaching Programme for Mentors of Beginning Teachers, *Journal of In-service Education*, Vol 2

Useful website

www.teach.gov.uk

This site gives access to a variety of links relating to both QTS and Induction